THE BOOK THAT JAMES WROTE

The Book That James Wrote

Earl F. Palmer

REGENT COLLEGE PUBLISHING
Vancouver, British Columbia

To our three children and their life partners

Anne and Greg Welsh
Jon and Kara Diane Palmer
Elizabeth and Eric Jacobsen

First published 1997 by William B. Eerdmans Publishing Co.

This edition published 2004 by Regent College Publishing
5800 University Boulevard, Vancouver, BC V6T 2E4 Canada
www.regentpublishing.com

Views expressed in works published by Regent College Publishing are
those of the author and do not necessarily represent the official
position of Regent College <www.regent-college.edu>.

National Library of Canada Cataloguing in Publication

Palmer, Earl F.
The book that James wrote / Earl F. Palmer.

ISBN 1-57383-290-1

1. Bible. N.T. James—Criticism, interpretation, etc. I. Title.

BS2785.2.P35 2004   227'.9106   C2004-900555-3

Contents

Contents

Acknowledgments

The Book of James is a New Testament letter that has been misplaced and misunderstood for a long time. The book is a great book, and now we know that it comes to us from the very center of the first century before the destruction of Jerusalem by the Romans in A.D. 70. I believe its writer is the bishop of the struggling Christian church in Jerusalem. When I became convinced that this very James was the author of the Book of James, I then read its earnest discipleship advice with new eyes and new anticipation. This theological commentary flows out of my own discipleship journey with the practical words of James. His book is totally challenging and at the same time encouraging. It is a book of advice and also a book of hope because the advice has its origin in the good news of Jesus Christ.

I am grateful to many people in my life who have encouraged me in the writing of this commentary. I first presented expositional studies of James at the University Presbyterian Church in Seattle and also at the Center for Continuing Education of Princeton Theological Seminary. These experiences convinced me of the importance of writing a commentary on James for today's readers.

I appreciate the encouragement in all ways from my congrega-

Acknowledgments

tion in Seattle, my colleagues in ministry, and especially from Shirley, my wife, and our children. They have been my mentors.

Seattle 1997   Earl F. Palmer

Plain Talk

I will admit that some people say I make too much of this, that I complain out loud when I should just be polite and shut up. But here is my problem: I think the food we are supposed to eat is too politically correct and too far down the food chain to enjoy. Where has rump roast gone, and mashed potatoes with the little lake of real gravy on the top (or even meat loaf for that matter)? Where is plain lettuce in a salad that has no hidden tiny strings of sprouts or mystery nuts or those surprise flower petals? Instead, what do we have to choose from? Even chicken is now politically correct. I recently was served at a proper restaurant skinless and boneless breast of organically grown Oregon chicken Cajun-slow-roasted over mesquite bark and presented on a bed of Minnesota wheat. Can you imagine such an odd thing?

I do not want you to think that I am anti-gourmet at all. I love gourmet food, and I often eat a waffle at breakfast if no pancakes are available. I'll even go for English muffins if they are sliced nice and smooth. But what I am pleading for is white bread, generous butter, and Skippy peanut butter. It is about time!

But more than bean sprouts is at stake when this P.C. (politically correct) or S.C. (spiritually correct) expectation takes over at a college campus or in government or in a church. Have you found yourself unable to say something that you really wanted to say because what you were going to say does not now appear on the approved relevancy list of today's idea pacesetters? Have you found yourself deliberately using certain words just because they are now politically or religiously correct, and not because you really mean what they say? Do you know the code words that will signal that you are an insider with the group that counts most?

How do you feel about these questions? I bring them up because I think a lot of us are eating mesquite dried-out and scorched chicken on soybean noodles and telling everyone at the table how interesting the mingle of flavors is. We don't really like what we are eating at all, but then we cannot think of anything else to do when the table is crowded with people whose disapproval we fear.

I have a solution. Try your best to keep a prophetic distance from every fad, whether it is of food or of ideas. The prophets of the Bible saw themselves under the law and the gospel of God, and when they were good prophets they did not forget that for them the message a prophet needs to share comes from God. The result was that these men and women stood out as unique witnesses to their time and generation. When they remained loyal to the covenants of God they were both a real bother to their own contemporaries and also a real help. Since their words were not the rehearsed echoes of the powerful voices of the dominant culture, what they had to say was fresh and refreshing. Even the hard words were better because what they said was more substantive. Slogans require very little thinking; they are so readily available, and at very little cost of brain power or soul power. But a prophet who is thinking through an issue in the light of the covenants of God's law and promise must become totally involved in the journey toward life and living as well as words and speaking.

We who want to be prophets today also need to live, think, and speak under the authority of the Word of God. The Old and New Testaments are our sources: they are the check and balance over against the pressures of our own crazy ideas — and the pressures of other people's crazy ideas too. This Reformation standard for the source of our discipleship and our message will keep us a lot more healthy than is the case when I or my generation chooses our own special mold into which every text of Old or New Testament is forced to fit.

Of course, we all look at the Bible through our own eyes, and we have glasses too because of damage to our eyes that we have experienced throughout our lives. A person who has suffered from oppression of any kind always sees things through eyes affected by that oppressive experience. But what each of us must not do is to swindle ourselves out of a new discovery of the power and goodness of the gospel of Jesus Christ through an old unpaid debt in our own experience of life. This swindle happens when we insist that everything Jesus says and does must somehow solve our own felt needs. The gospel offers surprises that are both salty and joyous, and we discover these surprises when we risk ourselves to the lordship of Jesus Christ without demanding the right to ask all the politically correct questions. We make the best discoveries when we cease trying to ensure that the answers of Jesus always support the prearranged solutions that we so badly want, or think we want. I make the best discoveries when I quit trying to force every theme of the Bible to answer the questions I decide are the most important questions.

Right now there is a terribly dangerous thing happening out there among people who should know better. I see it in both the right wing and the left wing of theological and social movements. It causes people to jump through tight word hoops in order to win tenure at a university or to get ahead with the people who we think really count.

Decide that you won't belong to any P.C. or S.C. fad is my advice. Don't let a phrase formulate who you are. Use simple English and say what you really mean to say. Be yourself and stand in faithfulness under the only standard that can set you free. Be a biblical Christian, and that means keeping your eyes on Jesus Christ, because that is what the Bible by its own message and design encourages us to do. The Old Testament in anticipation, and the New Testament in witness, both point us to Jesus Christ, who belonged to none of the fads of his own time. Not even such a good friend and strong supporter as John the Baptist could make Jesus religiously, prophetically, or politically correct. We each need to discover what the Bible is really saying as we study and read and hear it for ourselves.

When you express your convictions, use your own words, not someone else's. Try to learn from the people around you as a good listener, because a prophet must listen as much as speak; but do not allow that something that people want, or think they want, you to do or say become the P.C. hoop that you obediently jump through. Maybe John the Baptist ate such strange food for this reason. But then, Jesus ate ordinary food to prove the same point.

I have one more suggestion — why not read the book that James wrote? This is the book of plain talk in the New Testament and one of the best cures for religious, political, or social straitjackets that I know. James is an original, and he has written a book sure to offend everyone in some way. But at the same time, his book points us to a good and durable cure for all doublespeak religion or lifestyle. I need his book, and I have written this theological commentary on James because I wanted to write down some of the ways that James has challenged me in how I live my life and in how I think about life.

His book has drawn me closer to Jesus Christ. James has challenged me to mean what I say and say what I mean and — best of all — to trust God's faithfulness and generosity.

All of these discoveries I made from a bishop in Jerusalem who lived at the midpoint of the first century and is best remembered for his plain talk.

Seattle 1997   Earl F. Palmer

Introduction

The Book of James has carved out for itself a special place in the New Testament, and that is because it is primarily a book of advice. It contains 60 imperatives in just 108 verses! Not many of us would like to read so much pastoral advice, which may be the simplest explanation why the Book of James is not quoted as often as other New Testament books in early church letters and teaching tracts. Nevertheless there come times in our life journeys when we welcome advice, and these moments loosen the resistance to almost all adult advice that we have practiced since our adolescent years.

Obviously the context of advice makes all the difference in our ability to hear and accept it and to learn from it. For example, if I am a downhill skier and I have the chance to get some advice on high-speed skiing from Alberto Tomba, the Olympic competitor, then I eagerly listen to him and observe his technique very closely. I remember watching a PBS special in which Itzhak Perlman was circled by a large group of New York teenagers from Juilliard School of Music. They listened with obvious delight and serious attention to this premier violinist as he offered them his advice on the instrument that they all shared a love for.

If we wanted counsel on how to keep our sanity during long periods of imprisonment, then Associated Press correspondent Terry Anderson could give advice that each one of us would respect. He told reporters in one interview that during his seven-year imprisonment in Lebanon he read the Bible fifty times from cover to cover. That comment should make even the most cynical person curious about the books of the Bible. Not everyone could convince most people that we should read the Bible fifty times in order to keep our heads clear. From many, such devout advice might be sincere and truthful, but would be missing an experience indicator, a validation from the roadway. Terry Anderson, who kept his sanity during seven years of isolation, has that validation, which makes us more open to his counsel.

The point is this — we need to be in the right mood for advice, and we need to respect the one who is offering the advice. What constitutes the right mood varies from person to person, but it is usually directly related to feelings of need and pain. When we hurt or when we have decided we really want to know something, then we are the most teachable. Then we listen most closely to the teachers we most respect; and added to that, in all questions of the heart we learn best from those with whom we feel the most personal resonance.

This essential resonance factor, or what might be described as historical/psychological validation, provides us with the most persuasive evidence that we have for assigning the authorship of this book to James, the bishop of Jerusalem. This is the James recognized in Acts 15 and Galatians as the brother of our Lord and leader of Christians in Jerusalem. Josephus, the Jewish historian of the Jewish wars, identifies him as the one martyred in Jerusalem in A.D. 62. Paul also tells us of him, in 1 Corinthians 15:6. Who else in the early life of the Christian church could possibly write such a book as the Book of James? With its stern advice and judgment references to the wealthy leaders in the Christian fellowship, the Book of James would require enormous personal validation and clout just to "make it" in the New Testament canon. Only someone who has been through what James has been through could write that we should "face up to trials with joy," and even go on to say that such trials produce deepened character within those who experience such suffering. He has earned the right to say such things.

We know from our own experiences of receiving advice and giving advice that only with personal validation are we in the right mood either emotionally or intellectually to hear such bold counsel. Otherwise we usually discount statements like that as insensitive platitudes. But if we know of the writer James and of his courage in the face of the tragic persecution of Jerusalem, then we are willing to learn from his experiences. For this reason the book has endured times when the church has avoided and ignored it, probably due to James's attack on the pride of power and wealth. James is a part of the canon of the New Testament even though its themes sometimes oppose the practices of many churches and persons who read it.

I agree with William F. Albright in establishing a date for this book at before the A.D. 70 fall of the city of Jerusalem. This letter comes from within the time of crisis but before the final Roman punishment, which included an attempted erasure of the city of the Jews, in which the very name "Jerusalem" was changed to *Aelia Capitolina*. James is in the city during the years after many of the Christians have been forced to scatter: Peter to Rome, John to Ephesus, Thomas to India, Paul as a prisoner to Rome. James has remained, and he writes his letter from the Christian fellowship in Jerusalem.

We are the benefactors of these pastoral words from James. The letter is well written, and the Greek usage is of such a superior quality that James may have had the assistance of a talented secretary who was fluent in the Greek language. But though the letter is written in first-century Greek, its thought is profoundly Jewish Christian; James uses the Old Testament method of wisdom proverb writing throughout the letter. His book could be described as a New Testament Book of Proverbs. Another feature that stands out is James's indebtedness to the sayings of Jesus. Though our Lord's name is mentioned only two times in the letter, more direct quotations and allusions to Jesus' Sermon on the Mount (Matthew 5, 6, 7) appear here than in any other New Testament letter. James offers the early Christians not only advice in the tradition of the Book of Proverbs but also a commentary on the teachings of Jesus that appear in the Sermon on the Mount. But most of all, James writes a book of Christian encouragement from the midst of the cumulative hardship and persecution that Christians are experiencing in Jerusalem and the Mediterranean world at the time. What we need to do now is to understand James's city and the Christians who lived their lives in that city just after the midpoint of the first century.

Chapter 1

Jerusalem

What was Jerusalem like when the first century began? The city is very old, but not as old as many other Middle Eastern cities. The Jews had lived in the larger region around Jerusalem from the time of Abraham, about 1800 B.C., and had become a nation around this city on a mountain ridge from the time of Saul and David, about 1000 B.C., onward. The story of Jerusalem is not a peaceful one; soon after David and Solomon's reign a civil war broke away the northern part of ancient Israel from its south. The north was then called Israel, or Samaria, and the south, including Jerusalem, was called Judah.

There was not only interior civil war, but also continuous assault from more powerful nations around Israel. The Assyrians destroyed the Northern Kingdom around 710 B.C., and later came the defeat and destruction of Judah and its grand city, Jerusalem, in 586 B.C. by the new Babylonian Empire. Following this defeat, a seventy-year period of captivity (exile) occurred, for many of the people were deported to Babylon. Then a new colossus, the Persian Empire, rose in the north; and with its defeat of Babylon, Persia decided that the remnant of Jews in exile should be brought back to resettle the city once again. Ezra and Nehemiah tell of this period of reestablishment. The Old Testament account of Jerusalem ends with the narratives of Ezra and Nehemiah around 444 B.C.

But the Jews continued to live in their city, though never at sovereign peace or without the interference of greater powers that surrounded them. In 336 B.C. Alexander the Great won major battles throughout the coastal nations of the Mediterranean world, and with that victory the Greek language was introduced to the ancient Middle East. This Hellenization of the Mediterranean region had a profound impact on the story of the Jews and early Christians. The Greek language of Alexander would thrive as the language of choice throughout the ancient world, and that would mean that a truly international language would be available and widely used by the time of the first century. People were by necessity bilingual; for the Jews that meant that they thought and dreamed in the language system of their Hebrew heritage, but they had some knowledge of the Greek language as well. By the time of the first century it was Greek that they used most of the time in public gatherings. This helps to explain why Paul shocked the people in Jerusalem when he suddenly began to speak to them in Hebrew (see Acts 22:1). He would usually have spoken in Greek, so the people were surprised at his speech in the ancient language of their fathers and mothers.

Finally the army of Alexander left, only to be replaced by other aggressive neighboring nations. One of Alexander's generals, Seleucus I Nicator, seized power in Syria, and the members of his family brought increasing pressure upon the Jews. The worst of these was Antiochus IV, called Antiochus Epiphanes, who was one of the most brutal tyrants of all time. In 168 B.C. he sacked the city of Jerusalem with such devastating cruelty that the remaining Jews gathered together as freedom fighters around Judas Maccabeus and his father, Mattathias, in order to oppose the tyranny of Syria. These brave Jewish patriots were successful.

Jerusalem was a city of intrigue by the time of the Syrian occupation. The Maccabean brothers were themselves in control of the Jewish nation following their successful revolt against Syrian occupation forces; and the Maccabean family, which was called the Hasmonean house, would hold a stormy kind of power over the city until the Roman era. The temple and its worship were reestablished, which gave added importance and power to an ancient priestly community within Jewish society. This priestly community, later called the Sadducee party, held a privileged position in the city.

Over against the growing power of the priestly party and their aristocratic supporters there developed a remarkable lay movement that was first called the Separatist Movement: the Pharisem. They were well-educated laymen who were suspicious and openly critical of the growing power of the Hasmonean family as well as the priestly Sadducee party. These laity become the Pharisee party of the first century, and at the time of the ministry of John the Baptist and Jesus of Nazareth they stood over against the corruption of the priests and the Jewish kings. They rejected what they thought were the self-serving biblical interpretations of the Sadducees and the grasping for power and wealth that they saw in the political successors of the Maccabean revolt.

What changed everything was the totally successful Roman invasion of the whole ancient world in 80 B.C. From then until the destruction of Jerusalem in A.D. 70, the Romans would rule with complete efficiency and unanswerable power. The philosophy of Roman rule was different than that of the Babylonians, Syrians, and Assyrians. As a matter of policy, the Romans did not interfere with local religion or local kingships, with one vital provision: provided that the peace of Rome and the authority of Rome was preserved. This Pax Romana enabled travel and trade to flourish between the different countries under Roman control. Roman taxation and Roman currency provided within the empire a better economic benefit to Rome than would the deportation of captive peoples, such as the Assyrian, Babylonian, and Egyptian empires had used. Because of this relatively enlightened policy, and because of Rome's clear military power, the principal institutions of Jewish society cooperated with Roman governors. Some of these institutions — primarily the house of Herod and the high priesthood — greatly benefited in wealth and land and power.

Not everyone was so agreeable to this new Roman era, however. The Zealot party was formed as a secret terrorist organization of Jewish activists who bitterly opposed Roman rule. The Essenes also emerged in this period and established their own isolated and esoteric community near the Dead Sea. Their answer to the invasion of foreign, Gentile occupiers was extreme separatism.

The one who benefited the most from this new era was a man who called himself Herod the Great. He and his large family would rule under the Romans for about one hundred years. Herod married Marian from the Hasmonean house and then ruthlessly destroyed every possible rival from that family, including his own wife. With a favorable nod from Roman authority, he became the founder of the house of Herod, which continued in power throughout the whole period until the Jewish Wars against the Romans ended the era. Herod accumulated a vast fortune and constructed at least four great palaces — two near Jordan, one in Jerusalem, and one at the Mediterranean Sea that he named in honor of his friend Caesar: Caesarea. St. Paul was kept a prisoner in the dungeons of this villa for two years as he awaited a hearing on the charges made against him by leaders of the temple.

Into this complicated city of people and history wise men came in the wintertime of a Roman taxation census and asked of Herod the Great, "Where is the King of the Jews to be born?" We are not surprised to hear Matthew tell us that all Jerusalem was troubled along with Herod at hearing this simple question.

This is the city that Jesus entered on Palm Sunday, and at the temple of the city he upset money changers who had found their own shrewd way to profit from Roman currency regulations. The Pharisees appreciated what Jesus had done because their enemies in the family of the high priest were the ones who had enabled this corrupt and controversial practice.

But Jesus Christ would not become the possession of any group: he would not even allow his own family, of which James was a member, to prescribe the meaning and practice of his ministry (see John 6). Jesus Christ had a larger kingdom to win and establish than any caesar or governor or king could ever imagine, and that new kingdom, with a new covenant, was not a territory at all but an eternal relationship. Jesus was no apparent match for those who arranged his death. Jesus died by the Romans' extreme punishment, death by crucifixion, but death could not hold this Jesus; and on the third day he won the greatest victory of all time: Jesus of Nazareth conquered death itself. Even the disciples of Jesus themselves could not understand their Lord's grand intention until he had endured the gravest tragedy and won the greatest victory. One of those won over at last to the good news was the brother of Jesus himself — the man called James (1 Corinthians 15:7). Following that victory of Jesus, the good news began to spread in Jerusalem and beyond its border. That is the next story to tell.

Chapter 2

The Young Church in Jerusalem

The Book of Acts gives us beginnings and middle journeys, but Luke's narrative tells only a few endings. We know of the death of Stephen and of James, the brother of John and the son of Zebedee, but what of the other men and women of the early church? Luke includes no account of the final days of Peter or John or Paul or Barnabas or Philip or Thomas or the women in the apostolic fellowship, or of James. The most helpful interpretive reason for these omissions is the date of Luke's writing of his Gospel and the Book of Acts, which is placed shortly after St. Paul's final journey to Rome as a prisoner.

Luke tells the story of the early church briefly and movingly. It is the narrative of real people in real places, and like most human stories it is unfinished.

We learn of the early beginnings of the church at the time of the Jewish feast of Pentecost (fifty days after Passover). Luke tells of the remarkable spread of the gospel among people as the church grows under the leadership of Peter, James, and John (Acts 1–7).

Chapters 8 through 12 of Acts mark a turning point in Luke's narrative, as pressures build within the city and opposition crystalizes against the church. Peter, the very Jewish Christian that he is, discovers the universality of the good news, and he shares the Christian faith with Gentiles, as does Philip. But conflicts emerge in the church between Jewish Christians, who are convinced that the law of Moses must govern all new believers, and non-Jewish believers, who are trying to satisfy that law and at the same time hold a centered faith in the gospel of Christ that is their hope. During this period Stephen and James the brother of John are killed, Stephen by an illegal mob action and James by the decision of Herod Agrippa I. Peter is also arrested by Herod, but he experiences a miraculous escape from prison. We meet the early Paul in these chapters, but at this point in the narrative he is only a marginal notation in Luke's account.

The next part of Luke's story is devoted to his great friend Paul: Chapters 13 and 14 tell of the journey with Barnabas and the success of that ministry among non-Jews.

Chapter 15 is the James chapter, which tells of the first great ecumenical council of the Christian church, during which the centrality and finality of Jesus Christ is affirmed by the whole church. Jesus Christ is the only total help for total need, and his grace is available for all who have faith, both Jew and Greek alike. James agrees with this decision and gives a sermon that Luke records in chapter 15. Paul, in Galatians, also narrates some of the background color of this decisive meeting of the early church, and he shares with the Galatians the same good news that Luke narrates in Acts 15.

The remainder of Luke's Book of Acts tells of the adventures of Paul and the churches in Europe and Asia Minor (modern Turkey). Chapter 21 narrates Paul's final visit to Jerusalem. He meets James again (Acts 21:18) and is arrested and sent to Caesarea, where he is under arrest for two years. At Caesarea Paul meets Herod Agrippa II and Herod's sister, Bernice. Finally, when Festus is governor, Paul is sent on to Rome as a prisoner.

Following the reign of Festus, A.D. 60–62, there was a brief lull in Roman authority before the new Roman governor, Claudius Albinus, took full control. In this brief period a conspiracy led by Annas the Younger, the son of the high priest Annas, illegally arranged for the execution of James, the brother of Jesus, in A.D. 62. We have this evidence from the *Annals* of Josephus (20.200). This means that the Book of James was written to Christians as a letter from Jerusalem, perhaps as a follow-up on the great council meetings of Acts 15. It may have been written during the time of Paul's imprisonment at Caesarea, which would explain why James does not mention the name of his dynamic friend, for that would endanger Paul even more.

How are we to understand the book James wrote — this salty and joyous book; this controversial book; this good book? Like his brother's Sermon on the Mount, the letter of James has a way of making everyone feel uneasy. It still makes us uneasy. How do we in our century, so many years since the last days of Jerusalem, understand his words and his advice?

Every reader feels an uneasiness about the Book of James, but the good news of the book is that James points to Jesus Christ as the Lord of the book. In that is the possibility of hope — not just relief for our uneasiness, but good news for our lives.

Chapter 3

A New Book of Proverbs

The way the Book of James is written has troubled many readers. The German scholar Martin Dibelius was confused by James: "The entire document lacks continuity in thought. . . . there is a basic difference between this text and the coherent discussions which make up most of the Pauline letters."

Indeed James is different from Paul, in the same way that most of David's songs and Solomon's proverbs are different from the letters of Paul. But this does not mean that Paul's writing has more integrity, or even more continuity, than the others. It is just that they are different in the *kind* of continuity they present.

What is important for us is to understand each kind of writing for what it is, which is the first step toward enjoying and celebrating each approach in its own setting. In this way, we hear different writers speaking with separate voices, each voice with its own inner logic and beauty.

Paul writes his letters as one continuous sentence, during which the apostle takes his reader on a breathtaking journey through the step-by-step development of themes and ideas. There are always detours, but Paul brings his reader back to the grand design. Reading Paul is exhilarating and intellectually explosive.

With James, the experience is more like standing with him at the edge of a lake. He takes a rock into his hand and throws it out into the lake. You see it hit the water and you watch as rings form around its place of impact. This is the way he thinks. He throws out a great thought, and as circles form around that thought we see James tell stories to illustrate it. Some rings are positive implications, while other rings are shadow themes, or opposites. James's way of thinking is in a profoundly Jewish poetic tradition rather than the Greek rhetorical tradition. Both are valid, though they are different. James's is the literary style of Hebrew parallelism, a poetic device I have described as the rings that surround every idea. Some are positive restatements and some are negative, or shadow, statements, but all reinforce the center point.

Each Jewish poet in the Psalms and the Proverbs writes in precisely this way. Some New Testament writers use the method too. John writes his first letter to the church in this way, as in 1 John: "God is light; in him is no darkness at all." Here we see the rock hit the water's surface with its statement about God as light, and the first ring around that center point is a shadow statement about darkness. John then tells stories to show how the fact that "God is light" impacts our lives and our discipleship.

Now add to this poetic way of thinking one more of the Jewish poets' favorite methods of writing (here a German scholar like Dibelius might really be confused!). Just when you have begun to organize a progression of great thoughts, James stands at the edge and tells you, "I think I liked that first rock I threw into the water early on in this book so well that I am going to throw another one just like it." Three times James throws into our lake his "warning against the wealthy" rock; and we interpreters, trying to organize his letter, may think that there is no continuity, but we are wrong. Just as psalmists repeat great themes over and over and in different ways, so James does the same. The continuity is in the lake, in the thrower, and in the way rings mingle. There are skipping rocks, too, that cut across the spreading rings. But there is a poetic wholeness in the centeredness of the rock thrower, who finds each stone from the same riverbed. When we who read it allow the Book of James its own form and method, the whole of it makes not only sense but good sense.

We who read the Book of James in the twentieth century must respect the way that James chose to write his letter to the Christians in his time and place. It is my goal to give close attention to the words that he uses as he writes and to try to see each paragraph in its own setting. We will endeavor to watch his great themes as they appear and reappear in the letter.

As I understand the book that James wrote, he presents at least three grand themes in his book; they are the rocks thrown into the lake. Each of these grand ideas is spoken more than once; in fact they appear and reappear throughout the book. The first of these great themes is James's teaching about the nature of faith. This man who is famous for his use of the word "works" *(erga)* is, in fact, even by his use of that word most of all concerned to explain for us the meaning of faith.

The second grand theme, of even greater significance for James, is his understanding of the nature and character of God. The third grand theme is his very definite and far-reaching understanding of the meaning of our day-to-day behavior as Christians. James is practical and specific in the way that he as a pastor portrays to us the meaning of our discipleship as believers.

My own understanding of the book interprets the pastoral advice that makes up such a large part of the letter as implication rings that surround the first two grand themes, like the rings surround the splash mark on the lake where a rock enters the smooth surface.

James follows the tradition of the Old Testament writer of Proverbs, the psalmists, and the prophets as he announces a major theme or teaching and then follows up the teaching with stories, figures, and parables that illustrate his theme in either a negative or a positive fashion. The exciting images and stories that James gives within his book are for his readers some of the most memorable parts of his total message. James's vivid pictures stick with us alongside the teaching themes. Even his word choices are more visual than they are abstract and ideological. Jesus taught in the very same way. Such teaching fills the reader's or hearer's mind not only with ideas and concepts, but with pictures and stories. All of this makes for a very Old Testament kind of New Testament book.

Chapter 4

To Twelve Tribes

"James a servant of God and of the Lord Jesus Christ, To the twelve tribes in the Dispersion: Greetings." (James 1:1)

This book is clearly a letter, but from whom and to whom? The writer, who is named James, identifies himself as a servant of God and of the Lord Jesus Christ. We have indicators in this brief greeting itself that the world is not a safe place for Christian believers, in that James does not give a location for either himself or the recipients of the letter. He is simply James, which is the Greek version of the common Jewish name Jacob. His friends who hear this greeting are called the twelve tribes in the scattering. This is a riddle to baffle the best agents of the Roman government or of the house of Herod or sect persecutors in the office of the high priesthood. It is impossible to locate the families and individuals and congregations that shall receive and circulate this letter because the "twelve tribes" are in reality long since vanished, except in traditional story and memory. James has chosen an ingenious hidden reference to any reader who would consider himself or herself as an inheritor of the

Abrahamic people and who is now therefore a member of those twelve tribes scattered somewhere in the world of the first century.

When James writes, the Jewish people have been in the gradual process of scattering since the time of the exile and even earlier. There are synagogues throughout the Roman Empire where ten Jewish males have organized themselves for worship and the teaching of the Torah, the writings, and the prophets to their children. These people would be logical recipients of this greeting; however, we know that the letter is circulated among Gentile Christian congregations, which are not easily identified with Benjamin or Dan. Yet they too, in light of the great meeting at Jerusalem that Luke tells us of in Acts 15, are people who can rightly be called the inheritors of the twelve tribes of promise. Is this, therefore, James's way of welcoming and reminding at the same time? He welcomes the non-Jewish Christians into the family of Abraham by this description; and at the same time he reminds them that they indeed, because of the covenant of the gospel, possess the legacy of the patriarchs, the prophets, and Moses as part of their own legacy that is fulfilled in the Lord Jesus Christ. Jesus Christ, the Messiah, is the one who draws together in himself the whole of that unique history and grants a new meaning to the tribes of promise.

This phrase is the first exciting image of the book. It reminds us of a grand house from which we are all scattered, Jews and non-Jews alike — scattered not only in a geographical sense (James throughout the entire letter never mentions Jerusalem, which is his city), but in a larger sense of "homeness." That homeness is found in the words that formulate the first sentence of the book: these origin and home words are "God" and "Lord Jesus Christ." The home James has in mind is a relationship he and his readers have with God. James here is in full agreement with St. Paul, who always sees the kingdom of God in the relationship terms of the kingly reign of

Christ rather than in geographical terms. We are in the kingdom when we belong to Jesus Christ, and in that relationship we are a part of the whole covenant history that also includes twelve tribes of real people who lived in real places. James honors his non-Jewish readers by this inclusion; and he also reminds them, and those who will later read his book, that all people who trust in God have an inevitable continuity with the history of God's original Abrahamic people.

But what does he mean by "scattered"? It means at least this: that there is a home from which we have our origin, and the key thought for James is that the home is first of all the relationship with the Lord of every place. James uses relationship language to describe himself, too. He does not say, "James from Jerusalem," but instead, "James the servant of God." I think that James is right, at a very profound level, to establish as of central importance the Lord of every geographical place as the true home from which we are scattered as a missionary people and as a journeying people. But I believe he is also right to tie us, who are readers of the letter, into a group of people who lived on actual fields and by real wells, near mountains that have historical names. The twelve tribes are not phantom people; they are real and historical, they lived and raised families and died and sang songs that their poets wrote. We have a continuity to, from, and with these twelve tribes. This means that there is something about the gospel of Jesus Christ that creates both the scattering and the finding. We need to scatter in order to fulfill the journey task and the missionary task, but we also need to come home. We need a letter from home that tells us of the Lord Jesus Christ and of his welcome-home greeting. We need to know that we have a tribe where our name is known and honored.

I think one of the most heartbreaking descriptions of a person in literature is Joseph Conrad's description of Lord Jim. This young sailor is far from his home in England, but he cannot — or so he at least believes — return. He feels that his cowardice at sea in a terrible storm has made him unworthy of the earth from which he came. Lord Jim needs to know of the one who is able to resolve our scatteredness and to enable us to come home without shame. The sadness of Conrad's great novel is that this young naval officer never realizes a way to find this resolution. He keeps the grief as his own secret and can never give it up. He becomes a man of honor but not of grace. If only Lord Jim could have met this James of the Lord. James can help such a wanderer as Lord Jim in the very simple and direct ways that he tells us of God. What he says about faith will help, too. His book is a book for wanderers, and it contains a map home.

Chapter 5

Joy and Peril

"My brothers and sisters, whenever you face trials of any kind, consider it nothing but joy, because you know that the testing of your faith produces endurance; and let endurance have its full effect, so that you may be mature and complete, lacking in nothing." (James 1:2-4)

James begins his remarkable book with a direct reference to the stress and dangers of the first-century world. As St. Paul urges the Corinthians to be steadfast, in his closing words of the 1 Corinthians letter (chapter 15), so James begins his letter with three words that do not seem to belong together — "joy," "peril," and "steadfastness."

He faces with simple directness the perils that his readers, like he himself, must endure. His word choice is strong; the severe word *peirasmoi,* "trials" (RSV), is the same word used to describe the "temptation" of the evil one against us and against Jesus Christ. The darkest meaning of this word conveys intense stress that is meant to break and destroy. Yet we are baffled and surprised to hear his coun-

21

sel that we should rejoice in the face of this harsh reality. His stance is a defiant and bold response that immediately forces us to check to see who would dare to say such things.

We know from our own personal experiences that from only a very few people among our acquaintances would we be willing to hear such advice. We demand validation and proof from the people who say such things. James advocates that we laugh and rejoice in the very presence of extreme danger, and James has the right to say such a thing because he lives every day alongside the danger that his words tell of. Within months of writing his letter this brave bishop of the church in Jerusalem will lose his life because of his faith. Because of this validation, we are willing to listen to his advice, perhaps surprised at what he is saying, just a little confused, yet nevertheless encouraged that he said it.

But James has a very important point to make. The very incongruity of joyful rejoicing in the face of peril becomes for him an odd but wondrous sign of the victory of God's faithfulness against every source of *peirasmos* (temptation) — the acts of people or of the evil one. James intends to teach his readers that we may rejoice because the dangers that assault our lives cannot destroy the faith that trusts in God. These assaults become a part of the lifelong authentication of faith. The word that he uses, *dokeo* ("test"), means "thinking through, attesting to." His point is that the stresses of the peril have their own part to play in the proving of the validity of faith.

The result of this proving is endurance. James the writer, like Paul the writer, makes use of a very earthy word to describe endurance and steadfastness. The verb form of this noun, *hupomeno,* means literally to "stay under" or "hang on." It is not a triumphalist word, but rather one emphasizing labor. We will endure, and that endurance is dynamic: it is daily, steady hard work, hard work that results in wholeness and completeness. James uses the word for "health" as his final word in his list of results. The New Revised Standard Version translates this word as "lacking in nothing."

James does not tell his readers to rejoice because of peril, but to rejoice because the perils of temptation and extreme threat cannot destroy faith. We are not thankful for peril, but we are thankful in the midst of peril for the faithfulness of God.

In these sentences we have met his first grand theme — the meaning and possibility of faith. We now turn to the theology of faith according to James.

Chapter 6

Faith That Matters

"If any of you is lacking in wisdom, ask God, who gives to all generously and ungrudgingly, and it will be given to you. But ask in faith, never doubting, for the one who doubts is like a wave of the sea, driven and tossed by the wind; for the doubter, being double-minded and unstable in every way, must not expect to receive anything from the Lord." (James 1:5-8)

Read the following slowly: "A week ago I saw a cat walking on the side of the road; suddenly it noticed me and turned toward me. I grabbed my gun and loaded it quickly because I was far from our camp in the lower slopes of Mt. Kilimanjaro."

Notice how the word "cat" changed its meaning as the sentence unfolded. At the beginning you may have read the word with only modest interest since we see cats every day. But when the geographical location was mentioned, then the cat in my story grew much larger for you, the reader. There is a word in Christian vocabulary that acts much like this, in that it comes in different sizes: it is the word "faith." In its simplest sense, this word means "to trust" in both

24

the Hebrew language and the first-century Greek language. But for James this word is so important that he will, in several different ways, seek to carefully explain the full and growing meanings of faith. Faith will become a profoundly rich and dynamic word by the time James has stirred up for us a few of the vast implications and possibilities of Christian faith.

I want to explore this *grand theme,* this great cat that James has introduced to us at the earliest part of his book, a theme he cannot seem to get off his mind as the book unfolds. We are the beneficiaries of James's persistent interest in this word "faith," because he helps us to fully understand how radically good Christian faith really is. He also warns us against all shallow and emptying approaches to this strong word, which describes the journey and the relationship we are privileged to have with God.

Our first encounter with faith is in verse 3, in which James affirms his validated experience that faith in God is not fragile nor easily destroyed. Intense pressures on our faith are not as destructive as we might have thought, and James tells us from his own experience that there is something about our trust in God that is actually strengthened through testing. Faith, by its very nature as the dynamic experience of trust, is actually strengthened when pressures force us to focus on the center where we have placed our faith. We may lose confidence in secondary confidence points, but the peril drives us toward our most storm-proof confidence point, just as a fierce storm gives us the incentive of danger, so that we search out the safest ground and the strongest foundation. In this way the peril, though not in itself good, nevertheless has a clarifying effect on our choice of priorities and may actually increase our faith in that foundation able to withstand the testing.

The virtue that becomes ours from this kind of testing is what both James and Paul called endurance, steadfastness: *hupomone.*

25

Philo, the first-century philosopher, called *hupomone* the queen of the virtues because it is the virtue that is able to last the longest. Fads and infatuations do not have this *hupomone* quality, but faith in God does.

James takes us by surprise when he talks about the durability of faith in God that is able to stay healthy in the face of perilous hardships. We think that we want ideal growing conditions for our children. We choose the best schools for this reason. When Jesus told the parable of the wheat and the weeds (Matt. 13), he addressed this natural protective inclination of all human beings. When the workers find weeds in among the young wheat plants they ask the owner, "Shall we pull up the weeds?" Jesus amazes us in the parable by the words of his owner of the field, "No, let the weeds and the wheat grow together. . . ." What a shock — and an unpleasant shock at that — for parents, teachers, molders of youth. Jesus is teaching that somehow our faith and our character must be able to grow and even to thrive in less-than-ideal growing places. James has learned this truth from Jesus, and he has seen it validated in the experiences of Christians in Jerusalem. He does not call the weeds good, because they are not. They pose a real peril for the young plants that are growing in the field. But James is convinced that faith in God's faithfulness is able to develop into endurance and health in just such settings. On this note James begins his book and his portrayal of the meaning of Christian faith.

One more vital word is introduced to the reader in that first discussion of faith: "let steadfastness have its full effect *(ergon)*." *Ergon* is a key word here and later in the book for James, just as it is a key word for Paul (as in Philippians, where Paul says, "Work out your salvation because God is at work in you . . ." [Phil. 2:12-13]). *Ergon* means work as an event, as for example in modern physics, where the English word *erg* describes a unit of work. The other work word in the New Testament is *kopos,* which means work as sweat and effort. What James means by the use of *ergon* here is that faith, as it is tested, produces endurance; and this endurance becomes a fulfilling and molding event in our lives. It works itself out into healthiness, completion, and maturity.

Faith is an act of focusing directly on God and asking him for help. This is the skill of faith: focusing on God. James introduces the word "wisdom," which in the Greek world of thought has the sense of the reason behind and within a fact or reality. But the word in the Hebrew Bible has the sense meaning of skill, as in its use in the Book of Proverbs. James's sentence sounds very much like the Book of Proverbs, in which we are invited to ask God for wisdom and in which our reverence for God as the only answer to the meaning questions of life is seen as the true beginning place of all wisdom:

> For learning about wisdom and instruction, for understanding words of insight, for gaining instruction in wise dealing, righteousness, justice and equity; to teach shrewdness to the simple, knowledge and prudence to the young — Let the wise also hear and gain in learning, and the discerning acquire skill, to understand a proverb and a figure, the words of the wise and their riddles. The fear of the Lord is the beginning of knowledge; fools despise wisdom and instruction. (Proverbs 1:2-7)

James invites his readers to ask for wisdom from God, and then he makes his strong focusing point. "Ask in faith not continually dividing possibilities and not in doublemindedness but in directedness with your attention focused squarely upon the generosity of God." When James introduces the word "doubt" into this discussion about faith, we must be careful not to misunderstand what he is saying. He uses the word *diakrino.* The root word *krino* means "to divide, to

judge." The prefix *dia* means "through," and therefore the most lit-
eral definition of the word is "to endlessly divide, or endlessly
judge." James warns us not to linger endlessly in the about-to-decide
mode, but to put our weight down and commit ourselves toward the
one great certitude that deserves it: the generosity of God.

The person who endlessly divides possibilities but never lands
squarely and simply at a resting point is like a wave that has no cur-
rent direction of its own, but is dominated by whatever wind is most
immediate. James teaches us that it is the essential nature of faith
that a risk has been taken and a decision has been made — my life is
settled upon God, who has won my respect. It means in practical
terms that I have focused my life on God's generous character. This
is faith for James. Our Lord said the same thing in the Sermon on
the Mount, when he warned his disciples against trying to serve two
masters at the same time.

Think of T. S. Eliot's Prufrock, with the endless decisions and
revisions that he makes every day before the taking of tea. What a
waste of focusing time! Poor J. A. Prufrock doesn't know where to
turn next, and so he goes through his life like the cloudy evening sky,
"etherized on a table." He is dominated by each new or old fad and
each old or new wave. Because he cannot decide on the biggest
long-term questions, he cannot make up his mind on small questions either. The style of life that James is here describing as double-
minded is the approach to life of a person who cannot decide and
therefore settles down adrift in nondecision about who God is or
what God is like. In this frame of mind, a person can never really get
around to asking God for help. This adriftness of the soul James de-
fines as the opposite of faith.

He does not mean that faith has no encounter with doubt, because he has made the testing of faith his very first description of
faith. What he warns against is not the testing that is an essential

part of all healthy doubt, which seeks real answers. Rather he warns us against that endless testing which refuses to risk and to become vulnerable in the face of truth that has won our respect. It is clear that for James the Christian's faith in God is a response to evidence that has convinced mind and will of the integrity of God's character. Endless doubt and double-mindedness is like the state of a person who refuses to be consoled in the presence of genuine care, who refuses to become a friend in the face of genuine friendship. Whatever the reasons, whether pride or despair, in endless doubt a person is unable to focus on the true character of God. James urges such a person to ask God for wisdom (skill) to trust God's faithfulness and goodness and to do it before carelessly squandering months and years of life with nothing to show for it.

1. Faith Alive

"What good is it, my brothers and sisters, if you say you have faith but do not have works? Can faith save you? If a brother or sister is naked and lacks daily food, and one of you says to them, 'Go in peace; keep warm and eat your fill,' and yet you do not supply their bodily needs, what is the good of that? So faith by itself, if it has no works, is dead." (James 2:14-17)

James stands by the clear water of our shared lake and once again throws the rock of faith onto the surface, to watch still more circles form around the grand theme that is so vital to his letter to the first-century church.

He now speaks in crystal-clear terms about the simple fact that faith is an event that happens. For James, faith in God is not a religious person's mood or a secret knowledge about God. If we have

faith the people around us will know that we have faith in God because they will see it happen. James uses the word *ergon* (work) once
again in his letter to show that faith works out into concrete endurance and concrete results in our daily lives. Faith is alive and it has its
own dynamic inner force, which flows out of the relationship we have
as servants of God and the Lord Jesus Christ. James is making a con-
nection that must be made between relationship and character. We
who as servants trust God and the Lord Jesus Christ will show our relationship inevitably in living out toward those around us what has
been lived into us by God's generosity. Jesus made the very same point
in his parable about the steward who receives the forgiveness of a large
debt and who, therefore, is expected by his master to extend the same
debt forgiveness toward his own debtors, who owe smaller amounts.
This is not a hard teaching or an impossible requirement. It is the profound and basic doctrine of evangelical ethics. We love others and we
are made able to love others because we have first been loved ourselves. We forgive trespassers because our trespasses have been forgiven. The proof and the sure evidence that our faith is alive, in both
the parable of Jesus and the Book of James, is in this simple sharing of
the good and generous gift we have received. When we share the gift
of God's faithfulness toward the neighbors nearby, we prove our own
belovedness and our own forgiveness.

We hear the echo of the Sermon on the Mount in James's teaching about this faith that works. Our Lord commands his disciples in
his teaching on prayer that as we pray for God's merciful forgiveness
toward ourselves we also forgive others as we are forgiven (Matt.
6:14). Jesus gives the command not as a burden but as a joyous proof
that we are ourselves forgiven. How can I know that I am forgiven?
How can I know I have received grace? It is by the act of sharing
grace toward the people in my life that I am fully assured of my own
belovedness. James makes this very point without a wasted word.

But he has a postscript to offer as well! His postscript proves that faith is a far more profound event than an intellectual curiosity settled or an idea agreed to and intellectually formulated. For us to agree that God is one is a true agreement, but it may not be faith, according to James. Even the devil knows that God is the Almighty One. The devil knows who God is and shudders at the realization. But the devil does not trust God though the devil knows the reasons to fear God. Faith is more than speculative realization. It is the relationship that becomes a living part of my whole existence; and that agreement of will, mind, and body is something far better. Faith dares to enter into the presence of God and trusts in the goodness of God. Faith does not shudder and cower with fear and rage because faith has discovered how kind God is; like Abraham, who was called the friend of God, all those who have faith become friends of God. In fact, we are such good friends that we are permitted to give away the very best treasures of God's house. It is this gospel discovery that is the source of all ethics in the Christian understanding of ethics. It is very important that we who interpret James's stern warnings about the need for "living faith" remember that fundamental to his portrayal of working, living faith is this evangelical source of the generosity of God's character by which he began his teaching on faith. It was the first rock he threw out onto the water surface.

The living faith that James describes here is not heroism on the part of true believers, but instead it is the quite ordinary and natural application of our day-to-day relationship with God.

Abraham, the father of Israel, and Rahab, the harlot who helped Israel, are the two people James cites as examples of living, working faith. The common element for Rahab (Josh. 2:1-21) and Abraham (Gen. 22) is that they trusted in God at intense and stressful historical crossroads moments. Rahab showed caring kindness to a group of hunted and endangered young messengers of Israel. She risked her own neck by her willingness to wager on the faithfulness of their God. Her act resulted in their safety and also in God's blessing. And from that moment onward we honor the tradition of risky support for any persecuted people.

Abraham's trust in God was at a moment of overwhelming personal stress. As Abraham and his son, Isaac, trudged up Mt. Moriah, he was like any other religious figure of his era. He was about to practice Molech — child sacrifice — which was the horrible but common practice of all ancient peoples in the world of his time. The one difference was in a sentence that Abraham spoke to his young son, who asked of his father, "Where is the sacrifice?" Abraham said to his son, "God will supply the sacrifice, my son." We do not know what went through Abraham's troubled mind that day, but what we do know is that God took Abraham to the edge of that terrible mountain altar and, at just the right moment, God interrupted Abraham with a totally new event. "Do not touch the lad!" God provides his own sacrifice, and that sacrifice will not be our decision to make. God himself in his own Son, Jesus Christ, will take our place. Abraham and Isaac ran down Mt. Moriah liberated from ancient religion, in which we men and women do brave things to win over God's pity toward us. Abraham discovered the wonderful goodness and kindness of the gospel on Mt. Moriah, the good news of God's love for us and for our children. From that moment onward the people of Israel would be the only people among their ancient neighbors to reject *asherah,* harm done to children for religious reasons. Child sacrifice is described throughout the Old Testament as an abomination (Lev. 20:1-5); and when Ahab in his corruption reinstated asherah, he was described with the severest of all judgement statements (1 Kings 16:33).

The first big event on Mt. Moriah is the grand interruption because of the kindness of God, and the second great event at Mt. Moriah is Abraham's discovery that he should trust in God because God is faithful and God is good. We are not surprised that at that wondrous meeting place Abraham became the friend of God, who believed God, because Abraham learned that God had been his friend from the beginning.

2. The Durability of Faith

"Be patient, therefore, beloved, until the coming of the Lord. The farmer waits for the precious crop from the earth, being patient with it until it receives the early and the late rains. You also must be patient. Strengthen your hearts, for the coming of the Lord is near. Beloved, do not grumble against one another, so that you may not be judged. See, the Judge is standing at the doors! As an example of suffering and patience, beloved, take the prophets who spoke in the name of the Lord. Indeed we call blessed those who showed endurance." (James 5:7-11)

James has one final faith rock to throw into his lake, a new statement of the theme with which he began the book. James urges his readers to be patient and to be steadfast. The word that is translated here as "be patient" (RSV) is a very interesting combined word, *makrothumeo*. *Thumos* means "passion, rage," and *makro* means "far or a distance away from." Therefore, the word can be translated "far from passionate rage." It is the word that means mellow, even, and therefore patient. Paul uses it in 1 Corinthians as a description of agape love — "love is patient." Interpreters of James's book always notice the salty and even radical nature of James's words, but here his word choices seem to come from another side of his personality as a bishop and writer to the churches. James counsels his readers to be mellow and patient like the farmer who waits out the growing season because he trusts in plants to grow when given a chance with the early and the late rain.

This becomes for us a portrayal of the restful side of faith, which knows how to relax as much as it knows how to work. St. Augustine wrote of this mixture of rest and work in his *Confessions:* "O God who is ever at work and ever at rest. May I be ever at work and ever at rest." James is expressing the confidence side of faith, which knows from experience that, given time, the promise will be validated because the Lord of promise is himself coming alongside with the promise. James reminds his readers of the reason for our confidence, which has its source in God's character as true judge, as the compassionate and merciful one, as the Lord of purpose.

James, the prophet of high-action faith that is dynamically involved in working out the implications of grace, now becomes the prophet of confident faith that knows how to relax and to wait for plants to grow in their own time. These two prophetic challenges go together, and both are necessary in order to produce whole and healthy Christian character. Action faith by itself can become hysterically involved and too nervous! We know about the dangers of faith that is too theoretical, but there is a form of urgency about ethical involvement that is not really Christian either because it lacks confidence in God's promises. James understands that the real secret to our relevance in the world is the gospel of Jesus Christ; and the real source of power for the Christian is not what we have and show in our activity, but the steady result of confidence that Jesus Christ is the one who has the power.

It is this assurance in James's analogy that makes us the most helpful and least manipulative in our relationships with people around us. This assurance of and confidence in God's ability to authenticate himself is what enables us to step back a few steps from people and to allow them the space to move and think and to experience their own journey.

In his teaching on patience, James also shares with the churches his conviction about the return of Christ. "The coming of the Lord is at hand." James knows that we as Christians (and this is true of us in the twentieth century as well as those in his century) live our lives on this side of the decisive center of history; that center is the ministry, death, and resurrection of Jesus Christ. The fulfillment of history, which is the sure hope of the future coming of Jesus Christ, is the next boundary. This means that our lives, and all of human history as well as cosmic history, are bounded by Jesus Christ, the Lord of history. We do not look forward with dread, in expectation of inky abyss, but with the confidence of meeting at the next boundary the same Lord whom we know here in our present journey. Because of this confidence we are able to genuinely rest, to be patient, and to endure (*hupomeno* is the word he uses again).

James encourages his readers to endure as the prophets and Job endured. Job remained steadfast in the face of intense physical stress, and even worse, the theological-emotional stress caused by his friends' bad advice. Job insists on arguing with God, and his friends tell him that he has no right to argue with God. Their only counsel is that Job should, in humility, repent; but Job wants more than that and holds out for a larger, more profoundly personal hope against their counsel. In the end, God scolds the advisors of Job, telling them, "You should have listened to my servant Job. . . ." The greatness of Job is that he not only endured, he endured with integrity and he trusted God enough to want to argue with God. The Book of Job, therefore, stands as one of the greatest witnesses in all of the Bible to the meaning of prayer, the meaning of faith, and the meaning of personal integrity. Best of all, Job is a book about the meaning of the faithfulness of God.

3. Faith in the Family of Faith

"Are any among you suffering? They should pray. Are any cheerful? They should sing songs of praise. Are any among you sick? They should call for the elders of the church and have them pray over them, anointing them with oil in the name of the Lord. The prayer of faith will save the sick, and the Lord will raise them up; and anyone who has committed sins will be forgiven. Therefore confess your sins to one another, and pray for one another, so that you may be healed. The prayer of the righteous is powerful and effective. Elijah was a human being like us, and he prayed fervently that it might not rain, and for three years and six months it did not rain on the earth. Then he prayed again and the heaven gave rain and the earth yielded its harvest.

"My brothers and sisters, if anyone among you wanders from the truth and is brought back by another, you should know that whoever brings back a sinner from wandering will save the sinner's soul from death and will cover a multitude of sins." (James 5:13-20)

James is concerned that the Christians who read his letter understand one more fact about faith: its communal nature. Our faith is like a doorway through which people around us are benefited. Prayers of faith are of concrete value not only for ourselves, but for others as well. This means that our trust in God benefits other people. James has here opened up the mystery of intercessory prayer, by which a believer in God reaches out toward human needs and brings those needs to God. It is clear from this paragraph that James believes in the efficacy of the prayers of believers. For this reason he urges the believers to stay in fellowship with each other in times of joy and in times of hardship.

James also unites the prayers of believers with the stewardship responsibilities that believers have toward the earth and each other. He instructs elders in the churches to pray for those who are sick, "anointing with oil." This reference to "anointing with oil" is a first-century reference to medical attention. Just as our Lord used this phrase to describe the medical attention given by the Samaritan to the wounded man in the parable of the Good Samaritan, so also here James advocates that the churches should care about sick folk and bring them to the place where they can be medically treated, and in all of this the believers should pray in faith for them. This earthy and practical note by James is totally in character with his other practical references to the Christians in matters of their relationships with each other. For James it makes perfect sense that our strong faith would cause us to find a sick person, get the best medical care we can find, and then pray earnestly and with a faith that trusts in God for his help.

James does not want the apparent impossibility or size of the crisis to intimidate our faith. To encourage his readers at this point he reminds them of the prophet Elijah, who trusted God and even the weather was affected.

What he does not want to see happen among scattered Christians is that we become isolated and lonely individualists who try to have faith in God separate and away from the people of faith. His counsel is that, in spite of the faulty fellowship that Job experienced from his friends, we should always risk the fellowship and therefore experience faith together with other believers. I was told early in my Christian journey to always "find the Christians." I now see that the advice comes from James as he writes from Jerusalem. We cannot make it alone, and we should not try to do it. We need the check and balance of other believers to keep us doctrinally and morally honest and sometimes, even like Job, to make us obstinate, but we also need brothers and sisters to help us experience the very best gift of all: the forgiving love of Christ, which other believers help us find and trust.

With these words James's faith portrayal is completed in this letter to the Christians of his century. The words still ring true in our century as well.

Chapter 7

Understanding God

James writes a letter of advice to first-century Christians, but it would be a major mistake if an interpreter of this letter were to see this book as only a manual of advice. James is a theologian, and he expresses his theology in the same clipped, no-nonsense style that he writes his advice. There are never wasted words; and though it is his method to repeat themes in the Hebrew tradition of literary parallelism, we as readers are always surprised, at our readings of each restatement, by the freshness and boldness of James the pastor-theologian. James unites whole-person ethical action with whole-person intellectual belief, and so he becomes a helpful model for all pastor-theologians who try to give counsel to other believers.

What this means for us is that James will not give discipleship exhortations without at the same time establishing each exhortation on his doctrine of God. It is what he believes about God that makes everything else fit together.

When I think of the parable of the lake as one way to interpret James the writer, it seems to me that James's portrayals of and affirmations about God are like skipping stones that cross over each great circle made by the stones he has thrown into the pool. In this way he speaks of each Christian faith theme while always referring to his theological beginning place. Each of the great ideas that fill his mind and the great thoughts that he wants to share depends on what James believes about God. Let us therefore track that skipping rock and the vitally important circles that flow in rings around his convictions about God.

I. An Implied Wholeness

James first of all calls himself a "servant of God and of the Lord Jesus Christ" (1:1). Readers of the Book of James will notice that nowhere in this book does the author make any direct reference to the Holy Spirit. The word "spirit" in a lower-case sense is used in 2:26 and 4:5, but not in the sense of the Holy Spirit as the third person of the Holy Trinity. Does this mean that James does not have a doctrine of the Holy Spirit? We could also ask the same question of St. Paul on the reading of his letter to Philemon, which also contains no reference to the Holy Spirit. The same is true of the second and third letters of John. But James, like Paul and John, does indeed possess a theology of the Holy Spirit even though his letter does not include direct references to the Holy Spirit. In fact James helps us to better understand the New Testament theology of the Holy Spirit. What James confirms to us is that the doctrine of the Holy Spirit is an implied doctrine and becomes the implied presence in all assurance texts of the Old and New Testaments. This is the way that our Lord explains the promise of the Holy Spirit in John 14: "He will teach concerning me." "The Holy Spirit is the bond by which Christ binds us to himself" (John Calvin). This means for us that Holy Spirit theology is not self-conscious, nor in need of elaborate and special particularized teaching about the

40

person of the Holy Spirit, since the ministry of the Holy Spirit is fundamentally to point to Jesus Christ and to assure us of the love of God. The Holy Spirit does not turn our eyes toward the person of the Holy Spirit, but toward the person of Christ. We cannot even say that Jesus Christ is Lord apart from the ministry of the Holy Spirit (1 Cor. 12:3). Therefore, when James speaks of our servanthood as disciples of the Father and the Son, by saying these simple words he shares a meaningful faith in the full triune nature of God. The question, "Do you have the Holy Spirit in you?" fundamentally asks of us if we are assured of Jesus Christ and if we belong to him by faith. When we are able to say that we believe in Jesus Christ and that we are assured of his love in us and for us, then we have said enough.

James becomes a helpful theological clarifier for the ordinary Christian on this very important point. Some Christians worry about questions of their own experiences of fullness of the Holy Spirit in their lives. They thereby become overly focused on what they imagine is the special ministry of the Holy Spirit, as if that ministry and work were separate from the believer's experience of God's self-revelation in his Son Jesus Christ. In a remarkable way, therefore, James, Paul in his letter to Philemon, and John in his second and third letters have helped center us on Christ by their very silence on the special ministry of the Holy Spirit. It is not that these books do not have a theology of the Holy Spirit; instead, the writers recognize that our warm and personal relationship with God the Father and God the Son is what in fact signals our warm and personal relationship with God the Holy Spirit.

2. Wisdom

"If any of you is lacking in wisdom, ask God, who gives to all generously and ungrudgingly, and it will be given you." (James 1:5)

"Wisdom" is the grand and honored word from the Book of Proverbs, and James decides very early in his book to introduce this word to his readers. The Hebrew word itself as it is used in the Book of Proverbs means "skill," and its meaning in the Old Testament has about it this sense of skill for living and journeying on the right pathway, which is the way of the Torah (law) of God. "Wisdom" therefore in the Old Testament is a dynamic word of the way and about the way. The Greek world also loved the idea of wisdom; *sophia* is the grand and honored word at the heart of the very word "philosopher," one who "loves wisdom." *Sophia* has the sense in Greek thought of reason for and reason of a thing or purpose. This means that to be wise in this classical Greek sense is to understand reasons and meanings. When the two meanings of the Jewish and Greek "wisdom" are joined together as they are in the New Testament usage of the word, the result is both intellectually exciting and pragmatically useful. Biblically then we can say that we are wise when we know the truth and when we walk the truth.

For James it is God alone who is the source of wisdom. He intends by his use of the word both meanings: the first-century Hellenistic sense of source for meaning and reason and also the older Jewish sense of the one who is the faithful guide for our roadway. God is the source of truth and God is the companion for the journey. James urges his readers to dare to ask God for wisdom, and he follows up the invitation with a clear and encouraging description of God's character as the Lord of wisdom, who is eager to share it. Can you

42

imagine yourself on the edge of a great trek through perilous terrain? What you really need is a clear and accurate map — or even better, a guide to accompany you who knows the way.

3. The Generosity of God

James uses a word here that the RSV translates with the English word "generous"; it is the same word used by our Lord in the Sermon on the Mount (Matt. 6:22), where it is translated "whole, healthy": "If the eye is healthy the whole body is healthy." The meaning of *haplous* is just this: whole, healthy, and therefore generous in that sense of the inner unity of healthy exuberance. James wants us to know of the enthusiastic and nonjudgmental willingness of God to give real help to anyone who asks for wisdom. We are lacking (1:4-5), but God is whole and he has more than enough to share.

This promise has an extravagance that reminds us of the Sermon on the Mount, when Jesus invited his listeners to ask, seek, and knock (Matt. 7:7), and then followed that invitation with the parable (Matt. 7:9-12) about the father who will not give a rock to his child who asks for bread, nor a serpent to the child who asks for fish. Even though we often fail and fall short as earthly parents because of sin, nevertheless, we give good gifts to our children. God, who is totally good, gives good gifts too — we can count on it. (Note that the analogy Jesus uses shows his expectation about the mandate of parenthood. We who are parents are expected to give good gifts to our children, not a snake for a fish and not a rock for bread. This parable sets before us the clear obligation of parents toward children and alerts every parent to the standard of judgment when we meet our maker.)

What stands at the core of these words that James uses to describe the kindness and wealthy generosity of God is the fact of

43

God's personalness as much as of the nature of his character. God hears and knows and understands our prayers for help. God is not surprised by our weakness and our needs. All of this good news is included in those early sentences of the book. What a sentence of hope and grace this is! What a sentence of witness to the friendly character of God! There is a simple directness about it, but also a profoundly rich psychological subtlety. The subtlety is found in these words: "no reproach. . . ."

There are gift givers who offer help to us, but they diminish our sense of self-worth at the same moment that they grant assistance. We are made to feel very small and very inadequate and very guilty for our needy requests. The result is that we receive help in a certain narrow sense, but at the same instant we are reminded so blatantly of our need that whatever self-confidence we might have had is shattered. "Here, butterfingers, I'll fix that tire, you just get out of the way." The flat tire is fixed, but the person who needed help is flattened. There are parents who are never able to really help their sons or daughters without leaving a sour taste: "You always foul things up anyway." They leave their child humiliated because of ordinary weakness of youth and inexperience, announced loud and clear by the helper. It makes us wonder about the long-term gain and the long-term loss of such an encounter. What kind of help was it after all?

James wants us to know that God does not need to humiliate human beings to preserve his own honor and dignity. God is good, and God is sensitive to the precarious balances of human personality and human dignity. This generosity of character is an all-important foundation stone to James's theology of God. This stone skips across the water and across each other circle.

The psalmist in Psalm 77 wondered if God is good; and so does every man or woman who grieves death, suffering, and persecution in our life journey. At those terrible moments we just need to know if God is good. We need to know what we may dare to ask. James has been on that very roadway of suffering, and therefore we are willing to listen to his words of encouragement. We know God better because of James. We know that wisdom has its source in God and that we may blurt out our need for the wisdom of skill to make it on a difficult roadway and the wisdom of meaning to endure the lonely night times of the soul. Best of all, we know from James that the Lord to whom we pray is wonderfully generous and that he helps without those side glances of disdain and mockery. God respects who we are and the journey it is ours to take. This means that the help of grace from God, according to James, not only meets the present needs of our lives, but does so with the good humor of a warm and generous moment.

4. God of Hope

"Blessed is anyone who endures temptation. Such a one has stood the test and will receive the crown of life that the Lord has promised to those who love him." (James 1:12)

In continuing his portrayal of the character of God, James uses the word *stephanos,* which the RSV translates as "crown." St. Paul uses the same word in Philippians to describe the crown that he personally looks forward to receiving from God. This word does not refer to the crown that a king wears, which is the word "diadem." This crown is the emblem of victory that an athlete is given after a race. Here James is telling his readers of the award ceremony, when the prize is awarded because of the victory of an athlete who stays in competition to the end of the race. James also unites this portrayal of faith with love. We stay faithful to God throughout the time of testing because we love God. We love God because we have discovered his love and faithfulness toward us in the times of testing.

We need to know these facts about the future of our life journey and the race before us for at least two very important reasons. First, we need to know that there is a boundary beyond which the trials of suffering and persecution and even death itself cannot go. The boundary belongs to God, and when we know this it makes all of the difference. This great truth is the immovable foundation stone underneath everything else. Every other reality gains its meaning from this sure reality that God himself has set a time and a place where the final and best judge speaks the final and best words, where he announces the names of those who have faithfully stayed the course of the race. This is the divine accolade, it is the weight-of-glory moment that proves the meaning of everything once and for all. Those who suffer in their journey need this one assurance; and if it can be really trusted, then suffering can be endured. In this promise from James we have a witness to the fulfillment of the very first sentence of the prayer that Jesus taught: "Thy kingdom come, thy will be done. . . ." Underneath everything stands the decision of God.

There is one more part to the promise, and that is the promise of divine reward and divine recognition. We need this assurance, too, because every human being needs at least one crown to wear. We may try very hard to suppress this normal human need for recognition of worth, but the inclination to do so does not originate from God. He is by nature an award giver, who never tires of the ceremony of awards. It is in his very character to confer honor and worth.

5. God Does Not Tempt

"No one, when tempted, should say, 'I am being tempted by God'; for God cannot be tempted by evil and he himself tempts no one." (James 1:13)

Temptation is a harsh fact of life that confronts every man and woman, girl and boy. There is a subtle angle about temptation as a human experience that gives it its special terror. The evil one tempts a person toward an atmosphere of mind in which the person makes bad choices, and these bad choices then have destructive results to the person. Temptation is an assault, but not an open and direct one. Temptation is an indirect peril that causes two kinds of harm: first, the various kinds of damage done by the bad choice itself; second, the inner damage within the spiritual dynamics of the bad choice. We see these two kinds of harm work themselves out in each instance of temptation, whether it is in the Bible or in a twentieth-century story or in our own experiences.

Cain was tempted to make a bad choice, and the murder of Abel resulted from that bad choice. But behind that drastic result was the distrust of God's goodness, which caused Cain to choose badly. Temptation always twists something that we desire into a harmful result. John Knowles's powerful novel *A Separate Peace* portrays how sinister yet masked temptation is, in the river scene in which a young boy is tempted by older boys to make a jump from a tree as a supposed initiation rite into their club. They know that the small lad cannot make the distance of the jump from a high tree to the river, but they tempt him with the offered group acceptance, which means very much to this lonely boy. His jump results in grave physical injury. On the surface of it, it looks like he harmed himself by a poor choice; but at a deeper level the readers of the novel know the whole terrible truth: that he was tempted to harm's way by a larger evil designed by the older boys. His modest desire for acceptance gave the tempters a deadly access to his personality and the power to cloud his good judgment. He lost wisdom perspectives that he should have had; if he had been wiser, he would have stayed away from the initiation rite.

James wants his readers to know one extremely important fact about God's character: God never tempts human beings either to virtue or to vice. Not only that, but we can never succeed in our own attempts at the temptation of God. It is evil that tempts, and it is the evil one who is described in the Bible as the tempter.

James explains the psychological access point in the dynamics of temptation as human desire that distrusts God's faithfulness and therefore chooses to break across the boundary of the law and gospel to gain something that seems good to us to have.

God has no need, nor does God have any reason, to deceive our minds or our hearts in order to gain some small temporary gain. We are meant to be whole in faith and in life. Temptation is a strategy that breaks God's rules about the creation of man and woman. C. S. Lewis saw this fact clearly in his satirical book about temptation, *The Screwtape Letters*. Screwtape, the senior devil, is baffled by the ways of the Enemy (God), as he writes to the junior tempter, Wormwood

But you now see that the Irresistible and the Indisputable are the two weapons which the very nature of His scheme forbids Him to use. Merely to override a human will (as His felt presence in any but the faintest and most mitigated degree would certainly do) would be for Him useless. He cannot ravish. He can only woo. For His ignoble idea is to eat the cake and have it; the creatures are to be one with Him, but yet themselves; merely to cancel them, or assimilate them, will not serve.

6. Good Decisions

"Every generous act of giving, with every perfect gift, is from above, coming down from the Father of lights, with whom there is no variation or shadow due to change. In fulfillment of his own purpose he gave us birth by the word of truth, so that we would become a kind of first fruits of his creatures." (James 1:17-18)

The portrayal of God's character continues to gather momentum in the Book of James. God is the God of light, and by his own good decision he creates. Earlier James described the eschatological future boundary that is ahead in the human story, as he told of the God who speaks the divine accolade. Now we hear of the great speech by which God has created us and granted to us our life purpose. The boundary is now clearly set at the beginning as well as at the end of history. Just as in astrophysics the sound of the big bang continues to reverberate in radio static throughout the universe, so in James the sound of God's creative word reverberates still. These words of James bear a strong similarity to John's Gospel, chapter one, and Genesis, chapter one. It was God's speech that broke the silence of Genesis with "Let there be light." James reminds his readers of that speech and, as in Genesis, calls God's mighty act totally good. God is the giver of good gifts, who has placed a grand purpose into creation. We as human beings are the first fruit of that grand purpose. Every human being needs to know this and to trust the amazing implications of God's mighty act, which provides one more encouragement to us to keep our sanity and our hope.

7. Jesus Christ Lord of Glory

"My brothers and sisters, do you with your acts of favoritism really believe in our glorious Lord Jesus Christ?" (James 2:1)

For the second time in his book James names Jesus Christ as the one who deserves our faith and as the one who is the Lord of glory. The Greek word *glory* means "fame," "luminosity" in its most basic linguistic sense; and throughout the Old Testament *glory* always has to do with the mixture of the majestic presence of God and the wholly otherness of God. We now hear the words of praise that acknowledge Jesus Christ as the one who deserves this word of divine majesty.

I think it is interesting that James speaks of Christ's worthiness and glory in the context of our necessary modesty toward each other. Because Jesus Christ alone is the Lord of glory, we are to reject the kinds of pretense and discrimination toward other people that depend on a working theory of our own personal superiority. The apostle Paul in his Philippian letter develops this identical argument in his great hymn to Jesus Christ. Paul tells the Philippian readers that they ought to care about their neighbors and reject the way of empty glory ("conceit" is the word used in the RSV). Paul then tells of the mind of Christ and the way that Jesus fully identified with all men and women by his death. Therefore, God has highly exalted Jesus Christ and has granted to him the glory. What a contrast between empty glory and that of Jesus! Through the way of humiliation Christ emptied himself; and by God's decision the glory of exaltation that Jesus deserves is granted to him alone. Christ did not have empty glory, but he emptied himself and God granted the glory.

The logic of James and Paul is the same. We benefit from knowing Jesus Christ as the Lord of fame and luminosity and wondrous presence. Because of his glory we are able to relax, without the need to impress other people with our "glory." This becomes for us a reason for humility and an altogether healthy antidote to pretentiousness or discrimination toward others. I know One who deserves the glory, so my head is not so easily turned by the lesser luminosities of life.

8. The Choosing God

"Has not the Lord chosen the poor in the world to be rich in faith and to be heirs of the kingdom that he has promised to those that love him?" (James 2:5)

The portrayals of God by James point to the God who chooses: "Has not God chosen . . . ?" (James 2:5). God chose by his own freedom, and therefore we are to remember this finality that God holds in his own hands. For James, this aspect of God's character should produce in us a respect toward people. It is a restraint, making us more human and less dogmatic about our own opinions concerning people or things.

James then calls his readers to the way of love, but he describes the love toward the neighbor as "the royal law" (James 2:8). Whatever else he means by this kingly title for the mandate about love, he has succeeded in showing us that love has the royal imprimatur, an imprint that has its source in God's character.

James agrees with those who know the oneness of God: "You believe that God is one, you do well, even demons believe and shudder" (2:19).

James upholds the fact of the unity of God's character because it is a bedrock truth that causes evil to shudder. It is a truth from the very law of God (Deut. 6). Nevertheless it must be for us a lived truth, and not only a catalogued truth. Why would demons shudder at the fact that God is one? The reason is that the implication of the basic unity of God is a devastating blow to evil. Evil depends on keeping truth compartmentally arranged and isolated. Evil wins a victory if it can block a believer from seeing the implications of God's goodness and faithfulness for the believer's own ethical behavior and interpersonal relationships.

Another aspect of the oneness of God profoundly frightens evil: the inner unity of God's character. Evil hopes for many gods, or divine realities, that can be played off against each other, so that bargains can be made to the benefit of evil. But if God is one, there are no cosmic spiritual rivalries that can work to the advantage of the bargainer. James commends the Christian believer who trusts in the oneness of God, but he calls for a whole-life involvement as our part in that trust.

God "yearns jealously over the spirit which he has made to dwell in us" (James 4:5). James combines a quotation from three Old Testament texts, Exodus 20:5, Deuteronomy 4:24, and Zechariah 8:2, to establish the critical significance of God's care for human beings. God is deeply involved in this care, with the quality of concern that is best described by one word: "jealously." This emotion-packed word shows the depth of feeling that God the creator has about the worth and importance of all human beings. The word is very anthropomorphic. We wonder at such a portraiture of almighty God; we may be shocked by the thought of the jealous God — not jealously protecting his own honor and dignity, but jealous to protect the dignity of ordinary human beings.

The word "jealous" appears in several places throughout Scripture, and in my view in each instance the intention of its use is to shock and surprise the hearer/reader. We just do not expect God to be so deeply concerned about issues large or small in a way that fits with this word. We expect a more abstract, theoretical ultimacy, with divine qualities on a grand and vague scale. But God is not like we expect. C. S. Lewis in his book *Miracles* writes,

> Men are reluctant to pass over from the notion of an abstract and negative deity to the living God. I do not wonder. . . . An "impersonal God" — well and good. A subjective God of beauty, truth and goodness, inside our own heads — better still. A formless life-force surging through us, a vast power which we can tap — best of all. But God Himself, alive, pulling at the other end of the cord, perhaps approaching at an infinite speed, the hunter, king, husband — that is quite another matter. There comes a moment when the children who have been playing at burglars hush suddenly; was that a real footstep in the hall? There comes a moment when people who have been dabbling in religion ("Man's search for God"!) suddenly draw back. Supposing we really found Him? We never meant it to come to that! Worse still, supposing He had found us?
>
> So it is a sort of Rubicon. One goes across; or not. But if one does, there is no manner of security against miracles. One may be in for anything.

9. The Only Judge We Want

James continues his portrayal of God with one more piece of the great puzzle: "There is one lawgiver and judge, he who is able to save and to destroy. But who are you that you judge your neighbor?" (James 4:12).

The word "to judge," *krino,* means in its most primitive sense "to divide." James warns his readers against assuming the judgment role over our neighbor. We are warned against saying a final word in summing up a neighbor since we then usurp the singular priority of God. Only God has the right to divide and to say the last word about any person. This is a good-news warning at its core because any final dividing task is too heavy a responsibility for a human being, and the gospel removes that burden from us as part of the wondrous implications of the lordship of Jesus Christ.

God alone deserves to be the judge, and he exercises this right in two ways, according to James. Only God is the one who destroys what should be destroyed, and only God is able to save. He is both the giver and the sustainer of the law, by which the standard has been been established that measures all of life. He also is the only one able to finally divide and say the final word about all of humanity, which stands underneath and before the law of God. This divine limitation on each of us as members of the human family keeps us mellow and more understanding toward our neighbors. When we know our limitation it makes us less harsh and more open to the kindly generosity of God toward both ourselves and our neighbors. I know that I cannot say the final *krino* word of judgment about my neighbor, and I also know that my neighbor cannot say any final word about me. Both of these truths are imbedded in the very nature of God's character and in the sovereignty of his decisions.

This is a releasing truth: we are members of the human family, who are intended to obey the law, not to create our own law or to set ourselves as the final judge of our neighbors. Every human judgment is penultimate in its most essential nature since only God may speak the last word. Only God may finally divide and decide about the destiny of the human family. James has given one more humanizing example that shows us that when we know the truth about God, that understanding always has a good effect on us and on the way we relate to our human neighbors. Here our theology of God has a most important formative effect on the way we feel about our own existence and the existence of others around us.

10. The Lord of the Boundary

"Be patient, therefore, beloved, until the coming of the Lord. The farmer waits for the precious crop from the earth, being patient with it until it receives the early and the late rains. You also must be patient. Strengthen your hearts, for the coming of the Lord is near." (James 5:7-8)

History is boundaried, and that boundary is not the timetable of events, but the person of Jesus Christ, the Lord of history. The Lord stands at the boundary of history, and the New Testament Christians live their lives from this future certainty. James gives us a simple yet breathtaking affirmation of the coming of Jesus Christ as the future boundary that makes all of the difference to the way we live our lives here and now. He tells a parable about the farmer who waits for crops to grow in the confidence that plants will grow with the early and late rains.

The farmer has something that the ordinary layperson might not: confidence in the powerful growth potential of the plants that have been seeded. The farmer through experience has this one advantage. The Christian, like the farmer, knows about the powerful hope that is hidden just beneath the surface of human history. That hope is rooted in the fact that history moves toward the grand boundary of the Lord of history. Jesus Christ gives meaning to the whole story because he stands at the beginning and at the end. He also accompanies us in the middle of history: "Lo, I am with you always" (Matt. 28:20). This assurance is one of the first affirmations that James makes about God as the generous Lord who helps us here and now (James 1:5).

11. The God of the Name

"Are any among you sick? They should call for the elders of the church and have them pray over them, anointing them with oil in the name of the Lord." (James 5:14)

James tells us that in prayer we are to speak the name of the Lord! God is personal, and it is in this mystery beyond every other mystery that the whole of Christian faith gains its meaning. The vast question of all human history is this: What is it that precedes the big bang? What is it that has formed the grand design of everything? What is the presupposition on which all Old Testament and New Testament hope is founded? In the Bible we discover the answer to that question. All hope, faith, and love is found very early in the Bible in the earliest presupposition, the Abrahamic and the Mosaic and the Davidic presupposition. That which created and designed the complex whole is able to speak. The God that made our ear can hear, the God that made the eye can see, the God that made the incredible mind of man and woman is able to think. Just as we have names by which we are called by those who know us and by which we call ourselves, so God has a name, which Moses discovered when he boldly asked God for a name: "I am who I am" (Exod. 3:4).

Everything in Christian faith, hope, and love begins here in the beginning point when Abraham meets the God of character, the God of promise (Gen. 12:1-3), and when Moses hears the name, and when David asks his shepherd God for help. There is faith, hope, and love because the Word behind the name "become flesh and dwelt among us . . . full of grace and truth" (John 1:14). It is only this beginning place that makes prayer possible at all. Because we meet the God who has character and who speaks for himself, we trust his promises, and we dare to pray.

Chapter 8

James the Pastor

The pastoral advice that James offers to those who will read his letter is framed within the larger context of James's answers to two very big questions: Who is God and what is God like? And what does it mean for a human being living in the stressful first century to have faith in God?

The most important counsel that James has to share as a pastor begins with and within the confidence that James has in God's generosity. James's very first pastoral concern, as we have already observed in this commentary, is to challenge the Christians of his time to put their faith in God and to trust in God's character in spite of the intense pressures of their cultural context.

As a pastor he also presents definite and focused advice on specific issues that he considers important for the Christians in the midpoint of his century. We who now read his book many years later will try to listen closely to James, the pastor, teacher, and prophet to the church in his day, and we will study his words in the cultural context of our time as well.

Chapter one first focuses on the faithfulness of God in a stressful generation. James then gives his own witness to the grace of God, and he challenges those who read his letter to trust in God rather than to live in the adriftness of double-mindedness.

Following this foundation building, which we have considered in the opening chapters of this commentary, James begins his pastoral counsel. I will list these pastoral concerns in the sequence in which they appear.

Pastoral Concern 1: The relationship of the rich and poor in the Christian fellowship

"Let the believer who is lowly boast in being raised up, and the rich in being brought low, because the rich will disappear like a flower in the field. For the sun rises with its scorching heat and withers the field; its flower falls, and its beauty perishes. It is the same way with the rich; in the midst of a busy life, they will wither away." (James 1:9-11)

James's concerns about the dangers of wealth form a theme that he discusses three different times in his book. In his first presentation of the issue of wealth and poverty, he speaks plainly to the larger question of long-term life values and their durability. James argues that durability does not come from riches; they fade away, and those who trust in such symbols of greatness fade away with them. The teaching of James reminds us of Isaiah 40 and also "The Magnificat" of the mother of our Lord (Luke 1:46-55). Both songs tell of the leveling that is at the heart of God's good intention toward humanity. Therefore, someone with or without wealth may boast before God with open hands that do not cling to human symbols of greatness as if they granted meaning to our lives. That open-handed stance is honored by God, and James challenges all who might be tempted by wealth to remember the warnings about the vanishing mirage of greatness that is the true nature of riches' apparent splendor. We are to remember to test the durability of every value we choose.

Pastoral Concern 2: Temptation and desire

"Blessed is anyone who endures temptation. Such a one has stood the test and will receive the crown of life that the Lord has promised to those who love him. No one, when tempted, should say, 'I am being tempted by God'; for God cannot be tempted by evil and he himself tempts no one. But one is tempted by one's own desire, being lured and enticed by it; then, when that desire has conceived, it gives birth to sin, and that sin, when it is fully grown, gives birth to death." (James 1:12-15)

James teaches the most important truth about temptation, that God does not tempt us but that temptation has its origin in the nature of sin and our own desires. Later James will more completely develop this teaching about the temptation of runaway desires. He unites here in a preliminary way his understanding of temptation as bad decisions that human beings make because of *evil* and runaway desire. This combined source, desire and evil, will appear in later pastoral concerns of James, and with the intensification of evil beyond the generic sense here presented and toward the more concrete sense of the evil one, the devil. James will later show that it is the devil who is the tempter, as in James 4:7. Like other New Testament writers, James recognizes the reality of moral personal will against the will of God at the cosmic level of existence. This moral personal will against God is the devil, the evil one, the slanderer, Satan. A mysterious part of human freedom is that we are the deciders, who make decisions guiding our lives as a rudder on a ship guides the course of the ship. The book James has written makes little real sense without our recognition of the real nature of the decisions we make throughout our lives. We decide and we are deciders every single day. The whole of James's pastoral advice is founded on his recognition of the importance of our decisions. The power of evil resides in the possibility of temptation, and nothing beyond that, because the power of God's redemption won for us in Jesus Christ is a greater power. God's power in our favor produces steadfastness in us (James 1:2-3), and not terror in the face of the tempter. James faces up to the reality of the evil one as the tempter, but he is not in any sense preoccupied with the devil because of his confidence in the greater power of God's faithfulness. For this reason he is able later to say, "Resist the devil and he will flee from you" (James 4:7).

Pastoral Concern 3:
The importance of knowing the truth

"Do not be deceived, my beloved. Every generous act of giving, with every perfect gift, is from above, coming down from the Father of lights, with whom there is no variation or shadow due to change. In fulfillment of his own purpose he gave us birth by the word of truth, so that we would become a kind of first fruits of his creatures." (James 1:16-18)

James affirms the righteous character of God, and from this profoundly important height he wants the ordinary Christians who read his book to realize their destiny as a "first fruits" of God's mighty purpose. These readers are beloved brothers and sisters, and James does not want them to sell short their destiny as the inheritors of the good endowment from God. In these words James sounds a note that is identical in theological goal to the opening chapters of Ephesians. St. Paul's grand portrayal of our destiny as ordinary believers in Jesus Christ has the same quality as these words of James (Eph. 1:7-14).

Both Paul and James see this exciting first-fruits reality about our lives as Christian believers. I believe that James, like Paul, is wise to show to his readers this vast larger picture because we are tempted to feel our own smallness and inadequacy in facing a time in which believers are a tiny minority movement. There is a grander scale of values that is in fact the true shape of reality, and each believer needs to know this durable reality. How else can we choose against the false gods and the no-gods of what appear to be the powerful majorities in our own generation?

Pastoral Concern 4: The temptation of words

"You must understand this, my beloved: let everyone be quick to listen, slow to speak, slow to anger; for your anger does not produce God's righteousness. Therefore rid yourself of all sordidness and rank growth of wickedness, and welcome with meekness the implanted word that has the power to save your souls." (James 1:19-21)

James the pastor counsels his readers about the power of words and thoughts. He thinks through with his readers and with us the need for the Christian to be mellow in matters of our speech and the reaction that it causes. He counsels us to slow down our impulsive language and deeds, by which we speak and think and act too quickly. We should take the time to really become teachable and able to receive God's words that can save us and make us whole. He warns against anger (rage), which he reminds us is like a cancer with its runaway and ruinous destructiveness. He warns that we cannot achieve the righteous destiny of God's will for ourselves or for others by the means of rage. These words still ring true and are like a crucial litmus test of every revolution and every human advocacy.

When we use harm to achieve the goals of righteousness, we are like the one who hurts because he or she has been hurt, and in the end it is evil that wins the real battle in the summary of the day. "When we repay evil for evil then evil has won a double victory. First, it has hurt us in the beginning which was evil and then it makes us evil like it is" (Martin Luther).

James warns us against the temptation of zeal. He encourages us to slow down in the moments where fury is present so that the words that bring life and hope can have their powerful effect before the louder words of rage have destroyed hope.

Pastoral Concern 5:
Good words that become good events

"But be doers of the word, and not merely hearers who deceive themselves. For if any are hearers of the word and not doers, they are like those who look at themselves in a mirror; for they look at themselves and, on going away, immediately forget what they were like. But those who look into the perfect law, the law of liberty, and persevere, being not hearers who forget but doers who act — they will be blessed in their doing." (James 1:22-25)

James teaches clearly throughout his letter that faith is not a sentiment or idea but an event that happens. Biblical "faith" is a word like biblical "love" in the concreteness at the core of each word. Love is an event that happens, and so too is faith. James wants his Christian friends to know this bedrock fact so that the temptations of theoretical and abstracted Christianity do not happen to the believer. He worries about the person who may actually come to that odd place in life where we indulge in mirror watching and self-analysis, but lack any concrete repentance by which to do something real and definite with the interesting data we collect in our fascination with the mirror. C. S. Lewis has this kind of person in mind when his Screwtape gives the following diabolical advice to his assistant tempter:

> It remains to consider how we can retrieve this disaster. The great thing is to prevent his doing anything. As long as he does not convert it into action, it does not matter how much he thinks about this new repentance. Let the little brute wallow in it. Let him, if he has any bent that way, write a book about it; that is often an excellent way of sterilising the seeds which the Enemy plants in a human soul. Let him do anything but act. No amount of piety in his imagination and affections will harm us if we can keep it out of his will. As one of the humans has said, active habits are strengthened by repetition but passive ones are weakened. The more often he feels without acting, the less he will be able ever to act, and, in the long run, the less he will be able to feel.

We need James and his letter today because of our tendency to intellectualize ourselves and others, but to do it at a safe distance from real repentance or obedience in the light of what we discover. James warns us that thought or word without deed is fruitless (v. 26). There is no real fruit to eat from such a branch.

James concludes his pastoral advice with specific tests of reality that may seem to our twentieth-century ears quite peasantlike and oversimplified. James tells us that real piety consists of very ordinary and simple matters, like visiting orphans and widows in the places where they suffer: "Religion that is pure and undefiled before God, the Father, is this: to care for orphans and widows in their distress, and to keep oneself unstained by the world" (James 1:27). I think James is quite aware of the incongruities that sophisticated readers would notice in his stark and simple statement about piety. This awareness makes his words just as abrasively relevant to our high-tech generation as to the high-speed Romanized Mediterranean generation of his century. He has touched something deeply primeval and basic to our Christianity in the way he chooses to describe the reality of human attentiveness to God. In this primeval connectedness James becomes a pastor to our generation as well as to his own.

Pastoral Concern 6: A face to meet the faces

"My brothers and sisters, do you with your acts of favoritism really believe in our glorious Lord Jesus Christ? For if a person with gold rings and in fine clothes comes into your assembly, and if a poor person in dirty clothes also comes in, and if you take notice of the one wearing the fine clothes and say, 'Have a seat here, please,' while to the one who is poor you say, 'Stand there,' or, 'Sit at my feet,' have you not made distinctions among yourselves, and become judges with evil thoughts? Listen, my beloved brothers and sisters. Has not God chosen the poor in the world to be rich in faith and to be heirs of the kingdom that he has promised to those who love him? But you have dishonored

the poor. Is it not the rich who oppress you? Is it not they who drag you into courts? Is it not they who blaspheme the excellent name that was invoked over you?

"You do well if you really fulfill the royal law according to the scripture, 'You shall love your neighbor as yourself.' But if you show partiality, you commit sin and are convicted by the law as transgressors. For whoever keeps the whole law but fails in one point has become accountable for all of it. For the one who said, 'You shall not commit adultery,' also said, 'You shall not murder.' Now if you do not commit adultery but if you murder, you have become a transgressor of the law. So speak and so act as those who are to be judged by the law of liberty. For judgment will be without mercy to anyone who has shown no mercy; mercy triumphs over judgment.

"What good is it, my brothers and sisters, if you say you have faith but do not have works? Can faith save you?" (James 2:1-14)

The word James chooses in this section that is translated in the English text as "favoritism" is a word constructed from "face" or "countenance," added to the word "lift up." Therefore its meaning is to lift up our face over others around us.

His reasoning is this. Because of the grandeur of the true glory of Jesus Christ our Lord, how can we hold our faces above the people around us? Christ's true glory has made our self-glory such a small matter that we are foolish to put our faces above other men or women who like us stand before the true wonder of God's true glory. It's a little like a group of people standing together on a dock with their fish at the close of a fishing derby. One has a twelve-pound salmon, several with seven-pound, ten-pound, six-pound fish. One angler has caught a fourteen-pounder, and that competitor feels quite proud, until just at the last moment before the derby deadline a fisherman shows up with a thirty-eight-pound king salmon. By contrast every one of the others looks just about the same size, and whatever pride the catcher of the fourteen-pound trophy felt has been put into a new perspective by a winner, who needs no ruler or scale to prove which fish is the final winner in the derby. It's amazing how the conversation shifts after this catch is brought on the dock. In fact we would think it strange if the earlier apparent winner would try to draw attention to his or her penultimate triumph. In the same way James wonders how we can consider ourselves superior to others around us when we all surround the Lord of true glory.

Once again his pastoral concern is about the relationship of rich and poor folk in the Christian fellowship. He tells a brief parable-like story about a banquet and the places reserved at the feast for rich and poor. He shows his own grief about the oppression that some wealthy people have exercised against poor people, to such a degree that James almost forgets his earlier advice about the dangers of hasty anger. But at just the right moment James calls on the Christian fellowship to remember the Leviticus 19 expansion of the law about the love of the neighbors. He shows that we are not free to choose the laws we prefer, but we are a people under the whole of the covenant of God's will for our lives. He closes this warning against discrimination and partiality with the note of grace. God's mercy overcomes judgment, and in the depth of that grace James ends this part of his counsel. (Following this section James returns to a major consideration of the full meaning of faith, which we explored earlier in this commentary.)

Pastoral Concern 7: The power of words revisited

"Not many of you should become teachers, my brothers and sisters, for you know that we who teach will be judged with greater strictness. For all of us make many mistakes. Anyone who makes no mistakes in speaking is perfect, able to keep the whole body in check with a bridle. If we put bits into the mouths of horses to make them obey us, we guide their whole bodies. Or look at ships: though they are so large that it takes strong winds to drive them, yet they are guided by a very small rudder wherever the will of the pilot directs. So also the tongue is a small member, yet it boasts of great exploits.

"How great a forest is set ablaze by a small fire! And the tongue is a fire. The tongue is placed among our members as a world of iniquity; it stains the whole body, sets on fire the cycle of nature, and is itself set on fire by hell. For every species of beast and bird, of reptile and sea creature, can be tamed and has been tamed by the human species, but no one can tame the tongue — a restless evil, full of deadly poison. With it we bless the Lord and Father, and with it we curse those who are made in the likeness of God. From the same mouth come blessings and cursing. My brothers and sisters, this ought not to be so. Does a spring pour forth from the same opening both fresh and brackish water? Can a fig tree, my brothers and sisters, yield olives, or a grapevine figs? No more can salt water yield fresh." (James 3:1-12)

As we have observed earlier, James likes to revisit themes that he has explored earlier on in his book. James, as a pastor with advice for first-century Christians, writes in the same repetitious style as a writer of Proverbs, in the tradition of Jewish wisdom literature.

James has earlier in his book warned against the careless use of words (1:19-21); now he revisits his concern about the words that we use. He first challenges all teachers to welcome the check and balance of the content of our teaching since we "all . . . make many mistakes." Those who are teachers are held responsible for teaching, and therefore James's counsel to teachers becomes all the more urgent for them.

He creates parables: about ships and the very small rudder that guides the largest ships just as the human voice sets the course of a life; about a forest fire that is started by a simple, very small fire; about the difficulty a lion tamer would have in taming the human tongue: harder than the lions! about a mountain spring, making the obvious point that one spring cannot pour out at one moment fresh water and at another moment brackish water. These parables impress on us the importance of congruence in the Christian's words and works.

But what is most distressing for the religious person who reads this paragraph is James's portrayal of the possibility of destructive religion. James introduces to us that terrifying prospect of extremist actions that have a religious flavor: "We bless the Lord . . . and curse men" (v. 9).

Blaise Pascal said something that has always troubled me: "Men [and women] never delight in doing evil as much as if they can do it for religious reasons" *(Pensées)*. What a chilling thought. Pascal had in mind extremism that he saw around him, by which cruel people were able to do harm to other people while they visualized the advancement of a religious goal by such acts. But evil acts are evil acts, regardless of the reasons that we claim to justify them. This sixteenth-century Christian, Blaise Pascal, joined with James to call the terrible bluff of unrighteousness that wears a religious mask.

How can such things happen to us, and what is the cure? Extremism is a human condition of the soul that happens as a result of fear and the loss of hope. Fear and loss of hope happen when our confidence shifts away from the goodness and faithfulness of God, and in the loneliness and dryness of that disastrous shift, an odd sort of arrogance takes over our personalities, so that they are not checked and balanced by the gospel of Jesus Christ as Savior Lord. We overrate and overinterpret our own understanding of certain narrow themes, so that they become for us more certain than they deserve to be, and by that narrow standard we judge other people as our friends or foes. Everything then becomes very definite, and there is no room for complexity or the possibility of our own misunderstanding. This is the arrogance of the soul that causes us to harm everything we touch.

Extremism of every kind is one of the harsh winds that blows across the world's landscape today. Terrorists explain their acts with religious reasons in many parts of the world today, so that religion is joined together with tribalism and racism to justify harm done to people.

On February 7, 1993, in a special study of what the *New York Times* called worldwide "ethnic wars," forty-eight different conflicts in places such as Azerbaijan, Northern Ireland, Bosnia, even Fiji, were surveyed. We understand the dangers of extremism in our own lives. Anyone who has experienced domestic violence or riots or clashes of advocacy groups knows firsthand about the arrogance that results from fear and the loss of hope.

What is the cure? C. S. Lewis said that the "best cure for bad literature is a healthy diet of good literature." I believe that the same truth is the best and most realistic answer for the harm caused by all extremisms. We need a healthy relationship with Jesus Christ that will give to us that mixture of the faithfulness to truth and the generosity of love that are the marks of biblical righteousness. It is the gospel of

Christ that creates in us the quality and depth of hope that makes it possible for us to be models of hope in the complicated society where we live. It is simply true that the only way cultures and people change is as they see for themselves the durability and inner power of goodness at work in practical examples. The mountain springs in James's paragraph of parables need to put forth fresh water. These models of hope, in which ordinary people show in living situations that grace is more powerful than hatred, become for real people in real places the influence that really changes our lives and behavior.

Here is where we come in as people who are Christian believers. We have a person-to-person, model-of-hope strategy that really works in the desperate places where people have lost their hope. We have from the gospel an intrinsic modesty and mellowness that is one of the greatest marks of discipleship; according to St. Paul, "Let all people see your moderation [gentleness]; the Lord is nearby" (Phil. 4:5). When people around us see that stable and down-to-earth humility that comes from the gospel, they are themselves quieted and slowed down long enough to learn the source of hope. All of this is possible because the Lord is nearby. There is one scene in the *Chronicles of Narnia* by C. S. Lewis that I love as much as any other, and that is the grand ride of Susan and Lucy on Aslan's back just after the great golden lion has defeated death and despair at the stone table. There is no need to be afraid when we are on Aslan's back, and that safe place is the cure for every fear and every reason for the loss of hope.

James has given to us a very good word within his stern warning, the word "bless." The greater power of God's grace that causes the blessing needs to replace the lesser power of our crises that result from fear and pride. James tells us that this is what ought to be, and when it happens the extremist terrors are tamed and the springs produce fresh water.

Pastoral Concern 8: Wisdom and peace

"Who is wise and understanding among you? Show by your good life that your works are done with gentleness born of wisdom. But if you have bitter envy and selfish ambition in your hearts, do not be boastful and false to the truth. Such wisdom does not come down from above, but is earthly, unspiritual, devilish. For where there is envy and selfish ambition, there will also be disorder and wickedness of every kind. But the wisdom from above is first pure, then peaceable, gentle, willing to yield, full of mercy and good fruits, without a trace of partiality or hypocrisy. And a harvest of righteousness is sown in peace for those who make peace.

"Those conflicts and disputes among you, where do they come from? Do they not come from your cravings that are at war within you? You want something and do not have it; so you commit murder. And you covet something and cannot obtain it; so you engage in disputes and conflicts. You do not have, because you do not ask. You ask and do not receive, because you ask wrongly, in order to spend what you get on your pleasures. Adulterers! Do you not know that friendship with the world is enmity with God? Therefore whoever wishes to be a friend of the world becomes an enemy of God. Or do you suppose that it is for nothing that the scripture says, 'God yearns jealously for the spirit that he has made to dwell in us'? But he gives all the more grace; therefore it says, 'God opposes the proud, but gives peace to the humble.' Submit yourselves therefore to God. Resist the devil, and he will flee from you. Draw near to God, and he will draw near to you. Cleanse your hands, you sinners, and purify your hearts, you double-minded. Lament and mourn and weep. Let your laughter be turned into mourning and your joy into de-

jection. Humble yourselves before the Lord, and he will exalt you." (James 3:13–4:10)

The word "wisdom" in the Old Testament Hebrew means "skill," and it is in this essential *skill to be learned from God* sense that James includes this brief paragraph of advice to the first-century Christians.

He speaks of the importance of the meekness (disciplined directedness) of God's wisdom at work in the ways that we live our concrete lives. Over against this righteous context he shows the shadow side of the temptation to selfish ambition and bitter jealousy. We see in this paragraph that James is deeply concerned about the temptation of runaway desire in its combination with devilish unspiritual temptation. This is now the second time that he has sounded a warning about pride and self-referential arrogance to his first-century friends. He points up the good harvest that results from the wisdom we learn from God. What stands out in his list of virtues is the mellow, gentle nature of these fruits.

I read the novel *The Firm* by John Grisham, and one small feature in that murder mystery keeps bouncing around in my head. The main character, Mitch, is an impressive young man. He is number-two in his graduating class at Harvard Law School, and as the story begins we learn that he has two solid offers for a job after graduation, one with a Wall Street law firm where he had been a summer clerk and the other with a firm in Chicago. But a much smaller firm from Memphis, Tennessee, in fact wins him over, and he goes to work with them. What did it was the salary they offered, plus a mind-boggling package of benefits and financial incentives: a new BMW, a six-figure special annuity package, the payment of his law-school debts, down-payment assistance for his new house in Memphis, a $3,000 clothing gift, and generous funds for home furniture. In the middle of this avalanche of good fortune, only his wife, Abby, seems uneasy about it all.

She senses subtle inroads of control and domination that inevitably accompany such financial largesse. What intrigued me at the beginning of the novel was that such an outstanding person as Mitch could be so oblivious to the dangers of these financial hooks into his life. Then the answer came to me. He wasn't suspicious because he was convinced that he deserved the money they were paying him! After all he had been elected to Harvard Law Review and was second in his class. It made sense to him that the partners in the Memphis firm recognized his brilliance, and of course they were simply rewarding competence when they saw it. This dizzy self-confidence on the part of Mitch probably made him the second easiest person at Harvard to con and deceive, which is exactly what happened to this brilliant young man early on in this murder mystery.

I was relieved to know that the story of *The Firm* is only fiction and that real law firms do not and cannot really do what this Memphis firm did, but the story became to me a parable about how our pride and convictions of self-importance can get us into trouble and make us very vulnerable to just the kind of deception (perhaps on a smaller scale) that Mitch and Abby faced in Memphis. It is the deception that goes with greatness, either perceived or actual. It is the loss of the sense of my own ambiguity and my own humanity, so that I somehow feel above the ordinary folk who make up the rest of the world. It is the deception that because of my achievements I especially deserve rewards beyond ordinary reasonable boundaries, and it is therefore the deception that becomes one of the two main contributors to loneliness. The other cause is the opposite feeling, that I am so unworthy that I deserve punishments beyond ordinary and reasonable boundaries. Both deceptions isolate and confuse the soul of a man or woman.

When I look at life from the standpoint that, because of my own greatness, I deserve special and even luxurious benefits beyond the normal range of normal people, I have begun a journey toward the entrapment of pride and power. I spoil in myself the possibilities of the genuine surprises of grace because I too quickly define myself as outstanding and therefore fully deserving of every reward. This entrapment makes Mitch into a self-referential hero, intoxicated by power and therefore easily deceived by those who also have power. What a fool Mitch is in the early pages of the story!

The story also helped me better understand the no-nonsense approach that James takes in his letter. He plainly warns us against the temptations of power, and he boldly asserts that the appetites that are stirred up by those excessive expectations are the cause of war itself. "What causes wars, and what causes fighting among you? Is it not your passions that are at war in your members? You desire and do not have; so you kill. And you covet and cannot obtain; so you fight and wage war. You do not have, because you do not ask. You ask and do not receive, because you ask wrongly, to spend it on your passions" (James 4:1-3).

What is the cure for such dangerous pride? First, Mitch should have listened to Abby! When we learn how to listen to people who love us, we are on the way to a cure from the isolation of pride. From friends who know us, we often gain our early clues that some part of our life is in danger of spinning out of balance. I think this is one of the important roles that Christian fellowship plays in our lives. Second, we find the cure for the isolation caused by pride in the very same way we find the cure for the isolation caused by humiliation — we find it in grace. It is the discovery of God's love in Jesus Christ that makes us able to outgrow both false self-pride and false self-condemnation. These bad conditions are often a phase of our life journey, and it is God's grace that finds us and draws us beyond that phase into genuine fulfillment and maturity. The good news of God's grace helps us to recognize our ambiguities, to face up to our sins, to experience our belovedness by God; and in these three discoveries we are protected from the temptation to pride and the temptation to despair. Best of all, God's grace resolves our lives, gives us self-respect, and frees us up for real fellowship. These three are better by far than a BMW from the firm.

James makes the promise that the Lord will fulfill our lives in a better way than any firm. He uses the strong word "exalt" — God will lift you up to your proper height.

Pastoral Concern 9: The will of God

"Do not speak evil against one another, brothers and sisters. Whoever speaks evil against another or judges another, speaks evil against the law and judges the law; but if you judge the law, you are not a doer of the law but a judge. There is one lawgiver and judge who is able to save and to destroy. So who, then, are you to judge your neighbor?

"Come now, you who say, 'Today or tomorrow we will go to such and such a town and spend a year there, doing business and making money.' Yet you do not even know what tomorrow will bring. What is your life? For you are a mist that appears for a little while and then vanishes. Instead you ought to say, 'If the Lord wishes, we will live and do this or that.' As it is, you boast in your arrogance; all such boasting is evil. Anyone, then, who knows the right thing to do and fails to do it, commits sin." (James 4:11-17)

James warns his Christian friends to remember our common humanity in our relationships with neighbors. That constant memory will protect us from the arrogance of judgment toward the neighbor. Only God has the right to say the last word about any human being, and this fact will protect us from the sin of judgment. Paul makes the same point in Romans 8: Only Jesus Christ has the right to condemn, and Jesus Christ is the mediator. James calls us to be doers of the will of God, who stand under the law as do our neighbors.

He next turns his attention to another pastoral concern that is logically related to the pride of judgment. He challenges his readers to make plans about the future within the larger context of God's providence and purpose for our lives. James does not instruct Christians not to make plans or to live without personal goals in mind, but to make plans for the future fully aware of the temporariness of all human chronologies. He teaches us that our lives exist in time, much like a mist that is here and then passes from view. This means that our own time and space is not the permanent reality except for the covenant that God has made for and with and toward us. It is God's decision alone that guarantees the permanence of anything, whether the life of a human being or a kingly empire. Therefore James counsels his readers to make plans for the future within the grand wholeness of God's command: "If the Lord wishes, we shall live and we shall do this or that." We live within the kindly will of God; and within that eternal, durable purpose we make our plans and dream our dreams. These words of James are not bad news for the worth and validity of human life, but good news because of the goodness of God.

Pastoral Concern 10:
A warning against those who do harm

"Come now, you rich people, weep and wail for the miseries that are coming to you. Your riches have rotted, and your clothes are moth-eaten. Your gold and silver have rusted, and their rust will

be evidence against you, and it will eat your flesh like fire. You have laid up treasure for the last days. Listen! The wages of the laborers who mowed your fields, which you kept back by fraud, cry out, and the cries of the harvesters have reached the ears of the Lord of hosts. You have lived on the earth in luxury and in pleasure; you have fattened your hearts in a day of slaughter. You have condemned and murdered the righteous one, who does not resist you." (James 5:1-6)

Once again James has the dangers of wealth on his mind, and this time he is clearly concerned about the corrupt use of riches and the power of wealth that is used against those who cannot defend themselves because they are poor. He speaks plainly of fraud and dishonest treatment of workers. The words and the image pictures that he uses are directly taken from our Lord's words in the Sermon on the Mount (Matt. 6:19-24). The difference lies in the fact that Jesus warned his disciples against the dangers of a life that honors the treasures of wealth too highly. James has already spoken against that danger, and here in this paragraph he has in mind the final destructive stage of any obsession we might have with riches. In that final stage of moral decline, real harm is done to people who are exploited dishonestly in order to increase our riches. James gives frightening words of alarm and warning for any person who is tempted toward the corrupt use of the power that goes with financial wealth.

This warning task is one of the respected though not enjoyable obligations of the prophet, who has the privilege and obligation to spell out the implications of the kingly reign of Jesus Christ and the gospel. This is the salty side of the prophet's role in history. We prefer to hear the prophetic message of hope and salvation, but these stark words of sheer reality and justice are essential too: when we have really heard these words, then we are able to really hear and understand the words of sheer encouragement. If the gospel of hope is the last word, then these judgment words are the next to the last words. In an odd sort of way they too therefore become a part of the good news because they level the ground and clear away every pretension of human glory or human power. But such words cannot be easily spoken; and it is a simple psychological reality that we cannot hear them, really hear them, from just anyone. There needs to be a "right to speak" standard fulfilled before any listener can take them in and process them. James, the bishop of Jerusalem, has won that right to speak and therefore we listen — we squirm, we try to avoid their fury, but in the end we listen, and so they become a vital part of our whole journey toward the hope that is founded on truth.

Pastoral Concern 11: The art of patience

"Be patient, therefore, beloved, until the coming of the Lord. The farmer waits for the precious crop from the earth, being patient with it until it receives the early and the late rains. You also must be patient. Strengthen your hearts, for the coming of the Lord is near. Beloved, do not grumble against one another, so that you may not be judged. See, the Judge is standing at the doors! As an example of suffering and patience, beloved, take the prophets who spoke in the name of the Lord. Indeed we call blessed those who showed endurance. You have heard of the endurance of Job, and you have seen the purpose of the Lord, how the Lord is compassionate and merciful." (James 5:7-11)

God is faithful and God is good. It is the good and faithful Lord who is coming in his grand appearance to fulfill the human and the cosmic story according to God's own purpose. This is the theme of the eschatology of James (his doctrine of the summation). James calls out to his Christian friends to wait with creative patience for the Lord of the final boundary. The chief mark of this creative patience is described by James in story form in the parable of the farmer who waits for the fruit to grow from plants that are in the earth. This kind of waiting is well-informed waiting, because a fruit tree needs time and a skilled tender of plants who trusts in the growing. It means that for James we must not object to the small size of buds or shoots because such worries are both useless and uninformed. If the tree is alive and the buds are there, then we are wise to wait it out for their time to arrive. James's parable is a practical argument against the escapists who run away from dangers that are inflated and from resources that look so inadequate. He also warns against those who become distracted with meaningless arguments against other co-tenders of the crop; our chief responsibility as a farmer in God's field is to faithfully keep the plants watered and allow the growing to happen in its time. It is a creative and wise eschatalogical/future-tense stance that James the pastor has granted to first-century Christians as well as twentieth-century Christians. Our task is to be responsible servants of the Lord of the harvest and to allow the growing season its own timetable. This is very wise counsel for any Christian who is anxious about the faith journey, and especially about the speed or slowness of spiritual discovery that we observe in ourselves or others around us. For James there is no panic or excessive fretfulness in this stance because at its core he trusts in God to fulfill God's own grand purpose.

Pastoral Concern 12: Final thoughts

"Above all, my beloved, do not swear, either by heaven or by earth or by any other oath, but let your 'Yes' be yes and your 'No' be no, so that you may not fall under condemnation.

"Are any among you suffering? They should pray. Are any cheerful? They should sing songs of praise. Are any among you sick? They should call for the elders of the church and have them pray over them, anointing them with oil in the name of the Lord. The prayer of faith will save the sick, and the Lord will raise them up; and anyone who has committed sins will be forgiven. Therefore confess your sins to one another, and pray for one another, so that you may be healed. The prayer of the righteous is powerful and effective. Elijah was a human being like us, and he prayed fervently that it might not rain, and for three years and six months it did not rain on the earth. Then he prayed again, and the heaven gave rain and the earth yielded its harvest.

"My brothers and sisters, if anyone among you wanders from the truth and is brought back by another, you should know that whoever brings back a sinner from wandering will save the sinner's soul from death and will cover a multitude of sins." (James 5:12-20)

James gathers together in the final words the kind of advice that we would expect from a father or mother on the eve of a great leave-taking.

Echoes of the Sermon on the Mount continue with James's reminder to us of the words of Jesus that each of us should say what we mean and mean what we say. James himself has given to us a model of this kind of plain-talk integrity. He has spoken frankly to the Christians of his century, and he has dared to say exactly what he intended to say without smoke screens or double meanings or religious platitudes.

James calls upon the Christians to be totally honest about their feelings, whether of joy or of sorrow; and in the case of illness, he urges those who are struggling to get help in medicine and the prayer support of the family of believers. The anointing of oil is a first-century reference to medical treatment (note that in the parable of the Good Samaritan [Luke 10] Jesus makes the same reference to the anointing of oil as a first-aid treatment for the wounded man by the road). James urges the church to seek every kind of medical treatment and to pray earnestly to God for his help. In this context James shares his own pastoral/theological conviction that our prayers are honored by God. Prayer for James has real meaning within the space and the time frame where we live our lives.

His final word of advice urges the Christian to care about those who have gone adrift and have need to find their way home to the place of forgiveness and wholeness. On this note James abruptly concludes his pastoral letter to his century. If there were more words of farewell, they have been lost to us; but we are grateful for these that have been preserved for our New Testament.

Conclusion

For me the abruptness of the close of the book that James wrote is one more mark not only of his writing method but also of his life. This brave bishop of the ancient city that David built has been standing with us at the edge of our common lake. He has thrown rocks out upon the flat plain of the lake, and he has skipped rocks too. We have watched the rings form and spread across the water surface and we have learned about the large themes of faith and discipleship. James has been our teacher, and now he steps away and moves along to continue other tasks and face other challenges. It is almost as if he is interrupted before he can say everything that is on his mind. But then, in this he is like so many of the other writers of the New Testament and the other people of faith who become companions to us for a part of our own journey. We are fortunate to have known them and for the chances we have to listen to their words and to watch their lives. Then like James, without a formal and final benediction, they say farewell almost in the middle of a sentence. It was C. S. Lewis who told a young friend of his, "And besides, Christians never say goodbye." I feel this way about James and his book.

The Book of James and Martin Luther

"If the Epistle is 'of straw' then there is within that straw a very hearty, firm, nourishing, but as yet uninterpreted and unthreshed grain," said Johann Gottfried Herder in 1884. Martin Luther did not like the Book of James when he first read it: "It is a really dangerous and bad book . . . almost feel like throwing Jimmy into the stove." Later on he revised his opinion, perhaps after hearing of the commentaries of Calvin and Melanchthon, so that he had kinder words to say: "I think highly of James and regard it as valuable, although it was rejected in early days. . . ."

I think that in the early reading of James, Luther was distracted by his first interpretive opinion that the book had been written by James, the brother of John. But from this viewpoint it would indeed be difficult to make real interpretive sense of the book, because that puts the book so early that the letter ceases to be a general letter to the whole scattered church. When James, the son of Zebedee, was alive, the church had not yet been scattered. According to Acts, James, the Son of Thunder, died at the order of Herod very early in the Christian era.

Luther was also troubled by the themes of the Book of James,

84

and primarily by what he felt were major themes that were lacking in James, namely a strong evangelical message of salvation through the gospel of Jesus Christ. But Luther should have looked more closely, because the goodness of God's grace is a vital theme in James, along with his strong teaching on faith. James states these evangelical convictions in ways different from Paul's but very similar to our Lord's teaching in the Sermon on the Mount.

John Calvin may have been aware of Luther's reservations when he sided with St. Augustine in insisting on the importance of James to the canon of holy Scripture: "There are also at this day some who do not think it entitled to authority. I, however, am inclined to receive it without controversy because I see no just cause for rejecting it" (John Calvin).

Calvin goes on to explain the importance of the advice qualities of the Book of James by an analogy: "The writings of Solomon differ much from those of David; while the former was intent on forming the outward man and teaching the precepts of civil life, the latter spoke continually of the spiritual worship of God, peace of conscience, God's mercy and gratuitous promise of salvation."

James does not at first glance satisfy the evangelist Luther, but then neither would Philemon or 2 John, 3 John, or 1 Timothy. Each letter has its own goal as a part of the whole gospel; James writes his letter to believers who are in danger of going astray. Nevertheless, there are ways in which this letter resonates deeply with a man or woman who is not yet a believer. For some skeptics this book has had a very important evangelistic influence precisely because of the ethical advice, the advocacy for the poor, the rejection of all religious pretense, and the strong call to discipleship.

Detractors also spoke against this letter in the early centuries of the church, and in some of those instances it may have been James's strong position against the pride of wealth that caused the book's unpopularity. James, like Gandalf the wizard in *The Lord of the Rings,* is a stormcrow who gives too many warnings to be a favorite in the broad readership of the church. But the tenacious staying power of the letter, right in the face of this hesitation and open opposition, is one more very impressive example of the integrity of the early church handlers of the New Testament texts. They kept alive the texts as they had been given, even though those texts made the readers uncomfortable. The simple existence of this radical book in the New Testament is one more important reason why I trust the New Testament as a whole.

Appendix

Study Guide

The Book of James is a book of advice to Christians, written in a way that resembles the Book of Proverbs in the Old Testament. This first-century letter to the whole church comes from the Christians in Jerusalem and is written by James, who is identified in the New Testament as the brother of our Lord Jesus Christ (Gal. 1:19). These studies will focus on this remarkable book and also the Christian church as it existed in Jerusalem at the midpoint of the first century. I hope these questions and readings will aid your personal or small-group study.

Study 1. The Christians Who Stay in Jerusalem and Those Who Leave

Readings: Acts 6:8-15; 8:1-8; 12:1-17 — Persecution scatters the early Christians.

Questions for reflection: (1) As you read these texts, what clues do you find to understand the reasons for persecution of the early Christians in Jerusalem? (2) What effect does the persecution have?

(3) Why do you think it is that the pressures on the Christians do not destroy the fellowship and their growth in numbers?

Study 2. The Christians Agree on the Center of Faith, Jesus Christ Alone

Readings: Galatians 1:18–2:21; Acts 15 — Arguments between believers help the early Christians to clarify the center — or Christian faith.

Questions for reflection: (1) How would you describe the issues or conflicts that divide the early Christians? (2) What is the good result of this honest doctrinal difference of opinion? (3) Have you had experiences where an argument played a needed role in your own personal journey of faith?

Study 3. Paul Visits Jerusalem and Meets James a Second Time

Readings: 1 Corinthians 16:1-4; 2 Corinthians 8:1-7; Acts 21:1-26 — Paul brings an offering to the suffering church in Jerusalem.

Questions for reflection: (1) This offering is being collected for the relief of the saints in Jerusalem. What does that show us about the situation in Jerusalem? (2) How do you understand the words of James and the Christians in Jerusalem to Paul? What do you learn about these Christians from their words?

Study 4. The Book That James Wrote

Reading: James 1

Questions for reflection: (1) What do you learn about the peril of trials from this chapter? (2) What do you learn about the character of God from this chapter? Make your own list of James's portrayal of the character of God in this chapter.

Study 5. James and the Royal Law

Reading: James 2

Questions for reflection: (1) How does James explain the meaning of love? (2) How do you feel about the stories James tells to illustrate his teaching? (3) In what ways does James bother you? In what ways does he encourage you?

Study 6. James and the Meaning of Faith

Reading: James 2

Questions for reflection: (1) Has your understanding of the meaning of faith been challenged by chapters 1 and 2 of James? (2) How would you describe James's feelings about the Christian's relationship with people of different economic stations?

Study 7. Wisdom

Reading: James 3

Questions for reflection: (1) How do you understand James's illustration of the ship and rudder? (2) What are James's definitions of wisdom? What are for him the marks of wisdom in a person's life-style?

Study 8. Small and Large Crises

Reading: James 4

Questions for reflection: (1) How do you understand James's explanation of the origin of wars and large-scale conflict? (2) Why do you feel that he calls our lifetime a "mist"? What is his main teaching in that text?

Study 9. Patience and Action

Reading: James 5

Questions for reflection: (1) James repeats his concerns about those who are wealthy and uncaring. Why does he repeat his concerns? (2) What is James's teaching on patience? (3) In what ways does James call the Christians to proactive discipleship?

Printed in the United States
118216LV00002B/166-174/A